Pies

Pies

Josée Fiset and Dominique Boué

from Première Moisson Bakery

Fitzhenry & Whiteside

Table of Contents

foreword

Pies awaken wonderful emotions in me. From the indelible memories of my grandmother's pies to the many hours passionately devoted to the recipes in this book, pies, for me, are undeniably synonymous with pleasure, creativity and happiness.

For this reason, it was essential this book be as original, accessible and fun as possible; that it be a festive book. It had to make mouths water from preparation to tasting—why, even at first glance before making each delicious pie. Dominique and I have conceived the book in this spirit. We have gone to the extremes of our savoir-faire and imaginations, with an enormous appetite, to fill this book generously with our professional knowledge and creativity. Often, we've been inspired—by the moment, a photo, a curiosity, a cultural element or something else—and have let our intuition trump the rules of pastry making; we've pushed ourselves to be daring and innovative, to surprise ourselves.

I have gone through an entire summer conceiving pies, each as inventive as the last, to explore various sensory avenues, and have then served them to a tasting panel of volunteers. My children and their friends would immediately deliver their verdicts on my creations with exquisite frankness. What special moments!

We also had fun thinking outside the box while coming up with a multitude of pastry crusts and reinventing the pie. I think back to the times I brought out-of-the-ordinary homemade pie crusts to the office for my colleagues to try and exchange ideas about the best paired filling. I remember one particular morning when I arrived with a variety of pie crusts made with dried fruits held together with milk chocolate. What fun we had imagining what we could do with this idea from out of nowhere! Often it happened, purely from natural symbiosis, that I brought a new pie crust to work and Dominique found the filling.

What savoury adventures we have experienced in order to make this book a collection like no other! How many of our recipes did we start over again and again until we got results that lived up to our gourmet ambitions. More than once, and always to our delight, this process led us to a completely different pie than the one envisioned in the beginning. As we are apostles of choosing fresh ingredients, we invite you to take full advantage of seasonal harvests when you make your pies. Nothing beats the rich flavours of a filling made of freshly harvested fruit.

This book is the result of happy and excellent teamwork. Without the invaluable support of our colleagues, it would never have seen the light of day. Even so, this final product is an exact reflection of Dominique's and my vision. We have worked together since the beginning of the 1990s. Our vision, an insatiable passion for baking combined with our lively creativity, is a perfect model of us and is the fruit of a great bond. The pie crusts and pies presented, whether traditional or eccentric, simple or elaborate, rich or light, speak strongly for our unconditional love of gastronomy and our concern for healthy food.

Now that you have this book in your hands, our greatest hope is that it gives you an insatiable appetite for making pies and inspires you to invent new ones. Imagination allowed. Go for it and enjoy!

Josée Fiset

Pie Pastries

It is impossible to talk about pies without discussing the crust and consequently, the pastry. Pastry is the foundation of the pie, in every sense of the word. The crust can also be formed in many different ways. This book is proof. It contains more than thirty different crusts that you can fill to your pleasure. To honour tradition and begin this great adventure into pastry making, we first suggest our versions of the classics. Welcome to the marvellous world of pie making!

Short Pastry with Butter

The classic of all classics. In the rule book of Quebecois tradition, this pastry has always held good fruit pies wrapped in locally produced crust. Given the unforgettable memory of the smell, taste and texture of my grandmother's light, flaky crust, it goes without saying that I had to reproduce her pastry recipe in this book. Since my grandmother always eyeballed her measurements, I had to find a reliable resource to be able to reach my goal.

One beautiful Sunday afternoon in the country, my mother showed me how my grandmother made her pastry—without a recipe! My mother began by taking out ice to keep the water and butter very cold. We then measured all the eyeballed ingredients, which gave an authentic charm to the process. To ensure the ingredients remained cold, we did not handle them with our hands. We mixed them with knives, crisscrossing again and again until we obtained a coarse crumb. It was an intense exercise, believe me!

I have taken some liberties with these suggested recipes, the most important being the replacement of traditional lard used by my grandmother for butter. I have a weakness for the taste of pie crusts made with butter. It definitely came from learning to cook with butter with my mother and stepfather, a French baker. He put butter in everything and affirmed, "The more, the better." To accommodate different preferences, I have suggested two options. In the first recipe, the pastry is made by hand as in the good old days, whereas in the second, a food processor is used. Why not make use of modern advantages? In honour of my grandmother, I also provide an option that uses lard. It turned me into a complete addict for short pastry made with lard. Butter or lard? Don't count on me to decide!

Yields: Two 9'' (23 cm) crusts **Preparation:** 15 min
Resting time: 30 min

2 1/2 cups (625 ml) unbleached flour, cold
1 tsp (5 ml) sea salt
1 cup (250 ml) unsalted butter, cold
1/2 cup (125 ml) + 1 to 7 tbsp (15-105 ml) ice water, depending on the method you choose (see notes on page 12)

Method by Hand

- In a large, cold bowl, mix the flour and salt.
- Cut the cold butter into 5/8" (1.5 cm) cubes. Put them straight into the bowl and mix well to coat it with flour (image 1).
- With a manual pastry cutter or two knives, cut the pieces of butter while continuing to mix with the flour, until the butter pieces are the size of small peas (image 2).
- Add 1/2 cup (125 ml) of ice water and mix with a fork. Add ice water 1 tablespoon (15 ml) at a time, if needed, until the pastry begins to moisten and stick together (image 3).
- Form a ball with your hands, handling the pastry as little as possible (images 4 and 5).
- Cut the ball in two; make two 5" (13 cm) diameter disks. Wrap each disk in plastic wrap and refrigerate immediately for 30 minutes (image 6).

Food Processor Method

- Mix the flour and salt in the food processor bowl.
- Cut the cold butter into cubes and put them into the bowl. Use the pulse button to combine the ingredients until the diced butter pieces are the size of small peas.
- Add 1/2 cup (125 ml) of ice water and continue pulse until the pastry begins to moisten and stick together. If needed, add more ice water 1 tablespoon (15 ml) at a time.

- Form a ball with your hands, handling the pastry as little as possible.
- Cut the ball in two. Make two 5" (13 cm) diameter disks. Wrap each disk in plastic wrap and refrigerate immediately for 30 minutes.

To ensure that your water is cold enough, put cold water with ice cubes in the refrigerator for 20 minutes before using. Make sure not to pour the ice cubes into the flour.

To succeed at making your pastry, ensure that all your ingredients are cold, including the flour. The butter or lard will then have a better chance of staying firm throughout the mixture, which can only be beneficial to the quality of layers during baking.

It is important not to handle the pastry with your hands too much in order to prevent excessive gluten formation, which causes the pastry to harden and sometimes shrink during baking.

Variation with Lard

For those searching for a taste of the olden days and hoping to awaken food memories, simply replace butter with lard in the recipe. The quantity of water added to the pastry will be less than that for the recipe with butter (about 1 to 3 tablespoons or 15-45 ml). Note that the texture of the short pastry with lard is suppler than with butter. Because lard is softer, it is easier to mix with knives.

My grandmother, who lived on a farm, made her own lard with pork leaf fat. Leaf fat, also called caul fat, is the fatty membrane that surrounds the pig's tripe. According to my mother, who kept an indelible memory of the process, my grandmother removed the caul fat from two pigs that my grandfather slaughtered each fall. She put the fat into the oven overnight on low heat, about 150°C (300°F), to melt it slowly. In the morning, she collected the melted caul fat—the lard—and used it to make her pie pastries and tarts. She would then cook the caul fat that did not melt. For this last step, she would collect the golden caul fat from the bottom of the cooking pot and, in my mother's opinion, made the best cretons in the world with it.

My great-aunt Armandine didn't live on a farm and she said she made her lard with simple pork fat.

Notes

- Butter is harder than lard. If you're mixing by hand, it is easier to mix butter using a pastry cutter rather than knives. With lard, the process is easy with both utensils.

- The amount of ice water added to the 1/2 cup (125 ml) depends on the fat used (butter or lard) and the process chosen. Personally, I add 6 tablespoons (90 ml) of ice water when I make my butter short pastry by hand, 2 tablespoons (30 ml) when I make it with butter in the processor and 1 tablespoon (15 ml) when I make it with lard using either the processor or by-hand method. However, these quantities could vary depending on the proficiency with which the pastry is mixed. This is why it is important to proceed 1 tablespoon (15 ml) at a time.

Avoid rolling out the pastry too much when lining the pie plate. After lining the plate, chill the rolled-out pastry before baking in order to firm up the butter or lard. This will stop shrinkage and improve the quality of layering during baking.

With short pastry, it is important to begin baking filled pies on the lower rack of a preheated oven. This promotes the formation of steam, and consequently, layering.

Gourmet Note

With the scraps of short pastry, you could make nombrils-de-soeurs (recipe on page 146). You could also use the full recipe if you need a larger amount for a special occasion, such as a child's birthday party.

Whole Wheat Pastry

This pastry, made from oil and whole wheat flour, will please those who like healthier recipes. But any hope of layering should be forgotten because the fat content attaches entirely with the dry ingredients to form a smooth, homogeneous pastry. On the other hand, it allows interesting taste explorations. In the version below, I use canola oil for a more neutral taste. Using different oil—sunflower oil for example—will give your pastry more personality. Experiment with your favourite oils and have fun!

Yields: Two 9" (23 cm) pie crusts **Preparation:** 10 min
Resting time: 30 min

> 2 cups (500 ml) whole wheat flour
> 1 pinch baking powder
> 1/4 tsp (1.25 ml) sea salt
> 1 egg, beaten
> 1/4 cup (60 ml) water
> 1/3 cup (80 ml) high-quality vegetable oil

- In a bowl, mix the flour, baking powder and salt. Make a pit in the centre of the mixture.
- Beat together the egg, water and oil. Pour it into the pit.

- Blend the ingredients with your fingers until you create a ball of dough.
- Flour the ball, cover with plastic wrap and let rest for 30 minutes in the refrigerator.

Sweet Pastry

Prepared mostly with butter and egg, this pastry is thick and rich. The long baking time dehydrates it, giving it a nice crispy texture and a buttery flavour. By cooking the crust through, you maximize the flavour as well as the flakiness.

Yields: One 9" (23 cm) pie crust **Preparation:** 15 min
Resting time: at least 1 hr

> 1/3 cup (80 ml) unsalted butter at room temperature (semi-hard)
> 1/2 cup (125 ml) icing sugar
> 1 1/3 cup (330 ml) unbleached flour
> 1 pinch sea salt
> 1 egg, beaten
> 1/2 tsp (2.5 ml) pure vanilla extract

- In a bowl, mix the soft butter and icing sugar with a spatula until it becomes creamy in texture.
- Add the flour and salt. Crumble with your hands in

order to mix the flour with the butter until the mixture resembles sand. Make a pit in the centre of the mixture and pour in the beaten egg and vanilla. Gently mix in a circular motion with the tips of your fingers until a ball of dough forms.

- Flour the ball, wrap in plastic wrap and rest in the fridge for at least 1 hour (see Dominique's Advice and Note).

DOMINIQUE'S ADVICE

It is better to make sweet pastry and sweet chocolate pastry the night before. This way, it will have sufficient resting time and the texture will be at its supplest, without being elastic.

When these pastries are chilled, they will be hard to spread with your fingers. To make this job easier, allow the dough to come to room temperature or roll it out with a rolling pin.

Note

Sweet pastry and sweet chocolate pastry can be frozen. Just wrap them tightly in plastic wrap. Before working the dough, let it thaw in the fridge for a few hours.

Sweet Pastry Crumbs

Forget about store-bought cookies! Here is our house recipe for making cookies and transforming them into pie pastry. Work the dough twice and double your fun. You will not leave a crumb!

This uses the sweet pastry recipe outlined on page 13.

Method (to make the night before)

- Roll out the sweet pastry to 1 1/4" (3 cm) thickness and place on a cookie sheet.

- Bake until the centre is cooked at 325°F (160°C) for 20 to 25 minutes, or until the colour turns from golden to brown.
- Let the cooked pastry dry on the counter for 12 to 24 hours.
- Finely grind the dried pastry in the food processor to obtain sweet pastry crumbs.

Sweet Chocolate Pastry

This variation of sweet pastry is a delight for chocolate addicts like me.

Yields: One 9" (23 cm) pie crust **Preparation:** 15 min
Resting time: at least 1 hr

1/3 cup (80 ml) unsalted butter at room temperature (semi-hard)
1/2 cup (125 ml) icing sugar
1 1/4 cup (310 ml) unbleached flour
1/4 cup (60 ml) cocoa powder
2 pinches sea salt
1 egg, beaten
1/2 tsp (2.5 ml) pure vanilla extract

- In a bowl, beat the soft butter and icing sugar with a spatula until it is creamy in texture.
- Add the flour, cocoa, salt. Crumble with your hands to blend the flour and butter until the mixture resembles sand.
- Make a pit in the centre of the mixture and pour in the beaten egg and vanilla. With the tips of your fingers, delicately mix in a circular motion, until a ball of dough forms.

- Flour the ball, wrap it in plastic wrap and refrigerate for at least 1 hour.

Shortbread Pastry

Richer in butter and sugar than sweet pastry, this dough makes a flaky pie with a cookie-like texture.

Yields: One pie crust **Preparation:** 15 min
Resting Time: 10 min

1/2 cup (125 ml) unsalted butter at room temperature (semi-hard)
1/2 cup (125 ml) cane sugar
1 pinch sea salt
1 1/2 cup (375 ml) unbleached flour
1 tbsp (15 ml) baking powder
1 egg, beaten

- Mix the butter with the sugar and salt.
- Sift the flour and the baking powder twice to ensure they are well distributed.
- Add the flour mixture and the butter. Crumble.
- Add the egg and mix until a ball of dough forms.
- Flour the ball, wrap in plastic wrap and refrigerate for about 10 minutes.

Cookie Dough

This delicious and easy-to-execute pastry is truly similar to a cookie. It is neither a sweet pastry nor a shortbread pastry, but rather a crunchy pastry that resembles a British crumble. I learned how to make it thanks to Henri Marsand, a paternal member of my French family. He showed me how to make an apricot tart during a trip to Spain. We were in his apartment in Ibiza and the fruit had been freshly picked from apricot trees. Needless to say, my memories of it remain delicious and it gives me great joy to share this recipe with you on page 51. Pies made with cookie dough are simple to make and I have put together a few especially for this book.

Yields: One pie crust **Preparation:** 15 min **Resting time:** 10 min

1/2 cup (125 ml) cane sugar
3/4 cup (175 ml) unsalted butter, soft
1 1/2 cup (375 ml) unbleached flour
1 pinch sea salt

- In a large bowl, beat the sugar and soft butter with a spatula until it has a creamy texture.
- Add the flour and salt without handling the dough too much.
- Mix very little (about 1 minute), using your hands to form a ball.
- Refrigerate the dough for about 10 minutes. It should not harden.

Quick Puff Pastry

A classic in pastry making, this pastry always seems daunting to the uninitiated. But there is a quick method, based on short pastry, which provides similar results to a traditional puff. The secret is to fold the pastry repeatedly to obtain the much sought-after layers.

Yields: Two 9" (23 cm) crusts **Preparation:** 15 min

Resting time: 1 hr

2 1/2 cups (625 ml) unbleached flour, cold

1 tsp (5 ml) sea salt

1 cup (250 ml) cold unsalted butter, cut into cubes of 1/2" x 1/2" (1 x 1 cm)

1/2 cup + 2 tbsp (155 ml) ice water

- Put the flour and salt in a large, cold bowl and add the cubed butter.
- Using your hands, mix to coat the cubes of butter with flour without breaking them up (image 1).
- Make a pit and pour in the water. Gently mix until a ball begins to form (images 2 and 3).
- Shape the ball of dough with your hands, making sure to keep the pieces of butter as intact as possible (images 4 and 5).
- Flour the ball, cover with plastic wrap and let rest for about 1 hour in the refrigerator.

Turning the Pastry

- Generously flour the work surface, dough, and rolling pin when the dough begins to stick.

First Step (two turns)

- Roll out the dough lengthwise, 15" (38 cm) in length and 8" (20 cm) in width (image 6).
- Fold the pastry in three, like a wallet (image 7 and 8).
- Place the side of the dough with the visible layers facing you (image 9).
- Roll out the dough lengthwise again (same dimensions as the first time).
- Fold the pastry in three, like a wallet again.

- Wrap the dough with a tea towel or parchment paper and refrigerate for 10 minutes.

Second Step (two turns)

- Take the dough out and position the side with the visible layers facing you.
- For a third time, roll out the dough lengthwise (same dimensions as the first time).
- Fold the pastry in three, like a wallet.
- Once again, place the side of the dough with the visible layers facing you.
- For the fourth time, roll out the dough lengthwise (same dimensions as the first time).
- Fold the pastry in three, like a wallet, for the last time.
- Wrap the pastry in a tea towel and refrigerate for 30 minutes.

DOMINIQUE'S ADVICE

This pastry can be made the night before. To ensure it does not shrink during baking, cut the pie crust to the specifications of the recipe so it is ready for the filling. Let it rest in the refrigerator for at least 24 hours.

Gourmet Note

You could make sesame crackers with the scraps of puff pastry (recipe on page 146).

Traditional Pies

Pies create undeniable magic. The way some pies manage to trigger deep-rooted memories through smell and taste is fascinating. The most magical ones are, without a doubt, pies that are tied to our childhood—those made by our mothers and grandmothers. It is probably the reason most of us find these dishes so comforting, enveloping and reassuring. This first section highlights all the classic pies that make up our traditions as well as some that are part of the food heritage elsewhere. Made according to the fundamental rules of basic pastries, these pies dazzle with their simplicity and authenticity; although, we did take some liberties in reinventing some of them. After all, this pie-making adventure is truly related to creativity.

My Mother's Homemade Apple Pie

Servings: 6 to 8 | **Preparation:** 30 min | **Cooking time:** 55 min
Utensil: 9" (23 cm) round pie plate, Pyrex or ceramic

Ah! Mom's cooking just tastes so good. It has the je-ne-sais-quoi that comforts us and reminds us of all the love that has been doled upon us throughout the years. As a tribute to all mothers, I wanted to reproduce my mom's homemade apple pie. An easy recipe with a memorable flavour! The wonderful aroma of butter pastry—my mother was a butter devotee—apples, sugar, and a hint of cinnamon filled the house all at once. Thank you, Mom!

SHORT PASTRY CRUST

- Separate the short pastry in two and create two round balls.
- Flour the work surface and roll out each ball to make two round pie crusts, 11" (28 cm) in diameter.
- Line the pie plate with the first crust.
- Fold the second crust in two, make cuts with a knife and set aside.

FILLING

- Preheat the oven to 375°F (190°C).
- In a bowl, mix the ingredients for the filling. Pour the mixture into the bottom crust.
- Brush the edges of the pastry with water and cover with the other crust. Remove the excess pastry with a knife.
- Scallop the edges by pinching the pastry with your fingers. Brush the top of the pie with water and dust with sugar.
- Bake on the bottom oven rack for 10 minutes, then on the centre rack for 35 to 45 minutes until the crust is golden.
- Serve warm with crème fraîche or ice cream.

Blueberry or Raspberry Variation

- Replace the apples with blueberries, raspberries, or both! Simply add 1/4 cup (60 ml) of quick-cooking tapioca and mix with the fruit.

Out-of-Season Variation

- When seasonal fruits are not offered, it is always possible to use frozen fruits. To the previous variation, add 1 extra tablespoon (15 ml) of tapioca, or add an extra 15 minutes to the cooking time.

INGREDIENTS

SHORT PASTRY CRUST

- 1 Short Pastry recipe (see page 10)

FILLING

- 8 medium Cortland, Empire, Golden or Lobo apples, cored, peeled and cut into eight
- 1/3 cup (80 ml) + 2 tbsp (30 ml) cane sugar
- 1 tsp (5 ml) ground cinnamon

- 1 Short Pastry recipe
  (see page 10)

FILLING

- 4 cups (1 L) fresh
  strawberries, washed, hulled
  and cut in two
- 4 cups (1 L) fresh rhubarb
  cut into 1" (2 cm) pieces
- 1 cup + 2 tbsp (30 ml) cane
  sugar
- 1/3 cup (280 ml) corn starch
- 1/3 cup (80 ml) cold water

Rustic Strawberry and Rhubarb Pie

Servings: 6 to 8 | **Preparation:** 45 min | **Cooking time:** 1 hr
Utensil: 9" (23 cm) round pie plate, Pyrex or ceramic

SHORT PASTRY CRUST

- Separate the short pastry in two and make two balls.
- Flour work surface and roll out each ball to make two round pie crusts, 11" (28 cm) in diameter.
- Line the pie plate with the first crust.
- Cut the other crust into twelve strips, 3/8" (1 cm) in width, and set aside.

FILLING

- Preheat oven to 400^0F (200^0C).
- In a large pot, bring the strawberries, rhubarb and sugar to a boil.
- Remove the strawberries and rhubarb from the boiling liquid, taking care not to damage them.
- Set aside.
- Dilute the corn starch in the cold water and add it to the boiling liquid.
- Let it thicken for 2 minutes on medium heat.
- Carefully mix the strawberries and rhubarb in the liquid and let cool for 1 hour at room temperature.
- Pour the filling into the pie crust.
- Brush the edges of the pastry with water. Arrange the strips in a crisscross pattern on the filling and attach well to the edges of the pan.
- Brush the top of the pie with water and dust with sugar.
- Bake on the bottom rack for 10 minutes.
- Lower the temperature of the oven to 350^0F (180^0C) and continue to cook for 50 minutes, or until the strips are golden.
- Serve the pie once it has cooled.

Apple Blueberry Crumble Pie

Servings: 6 to 8 | **Preparation:** 45 min | **Cooking time:** 1 hr 15 min
Utensil: 9" (23 cm) round pie plate, Pyrex or ceramic

COOKIE DOUGH CRUST

- Preheat oven to 350°F (180°C).
- Place the ball of dough in the centre of the pie plate and spread it out with your fingers evenly from the centre to the edges.
- Place a piece of parchment paper on the dough. On this, put 2 cups (400 g) of dried peas (this step helps to keep the dough in place while baking).
- Bake the crust in the oven on the bottom rack for 10 minutes.
- Take it out of the oven. Remove the peas and the parchment paper.

CRUMBLE

- Preheat the oven to 325°F (160°C).
- In a bowl, mix the soft butter and sugar.
- Mix the flour and salt. Add it to the mixture of butter and sugar.
- Mix with your fingers until you have crumbly dough. Leave in large pieces.
- Place the crumble on a cookie sheet. Bake for 15 minutes or until the crumble begins to turn golden. Set aside.

FILLING

- Increase the temperature of the oven to 350°F (180°C).
- Heat the honey until it becomes liquid.
- In a large bowl, mix all the ingredients for the filling. Pour it into the pie crust.
- Sprinkle the crumble on top.
- Bake in the oven on the bottom rack for about 1 hour, until the apples are tender and the crumble is nicely golden.
- Cool before serving.

INGREDIENTS

COOKIE DOUGH CRUST

- 1 Cookie Dough recipe (see page 15)

CRUMBLE

- 1/4 cup + 1 tbsp (75 ml) unsalted butter, at room temperature
- 1/4 cup (60 ml) cane sugar
- 1 pinch sea salt
- 1/2 cup (125 ml) unbleached flour

FILLING

- 1/4 cup (60 ml) honey
- 4 medium Cortland, Empire, Golden or Lobo apples, cored peeled and diced to 1" (2.5 cm) pieces
- 3 cups (750 ml) fresh blueberries
- 2 tbsp (30 ml) corn starch

INGREDIENTS

PUFF PASTRY CRUST

- 1 Quick Puff Pastry recipe
  (see page 16)

FILLING

- 3 egg yolks
- 1/4 cup (60 ml) cane sugar
- 1 cup (250 ml) 35% cream
- 1 pinch ground cinnamon
- 8 medium Cortland, Empire,
  Golden or Lobo apples, cored,
  peeled and cut into quarters
- 1/2 cup (125 ml) raisins
- 1 egg, beaten

Apple Raisin Pie

Servings: 8 to 10 | **Preparation:** 50 min | **Cooking time:** 45 min
Utensil: 2" (5 cm) high and 9" (23 cm) round cake pan

PUFF PASTRY CRUST

- Separate the puff pastry dough into two equal parts.
- Flour work surface and roll out each ball to make two round pie crusts, 11" (28 cm) in diameter.
- Line the cake pan with the first crust and set aside the second crust.

FILLING

- Preheat the oven to 400°F (200°C).
- With a whisk, beat egg yolks and sugar until the mixture becomes frothy.
- Add the cream and cinnamon.
- Place the quartered apples and raisins into the pie crust.
- Pour the egg preparation over the apples.
- Brush the edges of the pastry with water and cover with the other crust.
- Remove the excess pastry with a knife.
- Scallop the edges by pinching the pastry with your fingers. Brush the top of the pie with the beaten egg.
- Cut out leaves and decorate the centre of the pie with the excess pastry.
- Lightly brush the tops of the decorative leaves with the beaten egg.
- Make a notch in the centre of the pie with the tip of a knife, then pivot to complete a circle and make a hole (a pie funnel) about 1/4" (5 mm) in diameter to allow the steam to escape.
- Bake in the oven on the bottom rack for 10 minutes, then on the centre rack for about 35 to 40 minutes.
- Cool before serving.

Pear on Chocolate Sauce Pie

Servings: 6 to 8 | **Preparation:** 30 min | **Cooking time:** 70 min
Utensil: 9" (23 cm) round pie plate, Pyrex or ceramic

COOKIE DOUGH CRUST

- Preheat the oven to 350°F (180°C).
- Place the ball of dough in the centre of the pie plate and spread it out evenly with your fingers, from the centre to the edges.
- Cover dough with parchment paper and place 2 cups (500 ml) of dried peas on top of it (this helps to keep the dough in place while baking).
- Blind bake the crust in the oven for 10 minutes.
- Take out of the oven. Remove the peas and the parchment paper.

FILLING

- In a pot, bring the cream to a simmer and add the chocolate.
- Stir until the chocolate is completely melted.
- Pour this into the pie crust.
- Place the quartered pears, with the tips pointing upwards, in a spiral from the outside to the centre.
- Bake between 60 to 80 minutes until the pears are golden.
- Cool to room temperature and serve.

OPTIONAL FINISHING

To make this pie glisten brush the pears with a honey topping (recipe on page 169).

Note

If the tops of the pears are too seared for your taste, cut the tips with scissors.

INGREDIENTS

COOKIE DOUGH CRUST

- 1 Cookie Dough recipe (see page 15)

FILLING

- 1/3 cup (80 ml) 35% cream
- 1 cup (250 ml) dark chocolate, chopped
- 6 medium Bartlett pears, ripe, cored and cut into quarters

JOSÉE'S RECOMMENDATION

Valrhona Dark Chocolate (66% cocoa) blends very well with pear; it is an excellent choice for this filling.

INGREDIENTS

SHORT PASTRY CRUST

- 1 Short Pastry recipe
  (see on page 10)

FILLING

- 1 cup (250 ml) 35% cream
- 1 1/2 cup (375 ml) brown sugar
- 1/4 cup (60 ml) unsalted butter
- 3 eggs, beaten
- 1 tbsp (15 ml) unbleached flour
- 2 tsp (10 ml) corn starch
- 2 tsp (10 ml) ginger, freshly grated
- 1/4 (1.25 ml) tsp sea salt

DOMINIQUE'S ADVICE

Keep peeled ginger root in the freezer; it will be easier to grate.

Ginger Flavoured Sugar Pie

Servings: 6 to 8 | **Preparation:** 30 min | **Cooking time:** 50 min
Utensil: 9" (23 cm) round pie plate, Pyrex or ceramic

The addition of ginger to this classic gives it a fresh taste that tickles the taste buds.

SHORT PASTRY CRUST

- Separate the short pastry in two and make two balls.*
- Flour the work surface and roll out one ball to make a round pie crust 12" (30 cm) in diameter.
- Line the pie plate with the crust.

FILLING

- Preheat the oven to 350°F (180°C).
- In a pot, heat the cream, brown sugar and butter without bringing it to a boil.
- In a bowl, whisk together the rest of the ingredients.
- Add the hot cream mixture. Beat everything vigorously until the mixture has a smooth consistency.
- Pour the filling into the pie crust.
- Remove the excess pastry with a knife.
- Bake on the bottom rack of the oven for 50 minutes without bringing the filling to a boil.
- Cool and serve.

* As this pie uses only half of the short pastry recipe, keep the other half to make another pie or more nombrils-de-sœurs (recipe on page 146). Wrapped in plastic wrap, the dough will easily last a month in the freezer.

Premiere Moisson's Pecan Pie

Servings: 8 to 10 | Preparation: 30 min | Cooking time: 45 min
Utensil: 9" (23 cm) round pie plate, Pyrex or ceramic

SWEET PASTRY CRUST

- Preheat the oven to 350°F (180°C).
- Flour the work surface, roll out the dough with a rolling pin and line the pie plate. Or, place the ball of dough in the centre of the pie plate and spread it out evenly with your fingers from the centre to the edges.
- Cover the dough with parchment paper and place 2 cups (500 ml) of dried peas on top of it (this helps to keep the dough in place while baking).
- Bake the crust for 20 minutes on the bottom rack.
- Remove the peas and the parchment paper from the crust and continue baking for 15 minutes in the centre of the oven or until the crust is cooked in the centre and is golden.
- Take it out of the oven and let cool at room temperature for 30 minutes.

FILLING

- In a bowl, mix the sugar, corn syrup and eggs. Beat well with a whisk.
- Add the corn starch and melted butter and mix well to obtain a homogeneous consistency.
- Place the pecans on the crust.
- Pour the preparation over the pecans.
- Put in the oven and bake for about 45 minutes.
- Let cool for 4 to 5 hours at room temperature and serve.
- To set the preparation more quickly, let the pie cool in the refrigerator.

INGREDIENTS

SWEET PASTRY CRUST

- 1 Sweet Pastry recipe (see page 13)

FILLING

- 1 cup (250 ml) cane sugar
- 3/4 cup (175 ml) corn syrup
- 3 eggs, beaten
- 2 tbsp (30 ml) corn starch
- 1/2 cup (125 ml) unsalted butter, melted
- 2 cups (500 ml) pecans

- 1 Short Pastry recipe
  (see page 10)

FILLING

- 3/4 cup (175 ml) cane sugar
- 2 tbsp (30 ml)
  unbleached flour
- 1 egg white
- 3/4 cup (175 ml) 35% cream

WHIPPED CREAM

- 1 1/2 cup (375 ml) 35%
  cream
- 1 tbsp (15 ml) cane sugar
- 1 tsp (5 ml) pure vanilla
  extract

DOMINIQUE'S ADVICE

This pie has a tendency to boil over
the pie plate when baking.
To prevent a mess, place a cookie
sheet under the pie plate.

Awfully Good Olden Time Cream Pie

Servings: 6 to 8 | **Preparation:** 30 min | **Cooking time:** 50 min
Utensil: 9" (23 cm) round pie plate, Pyrex or ceramic

A book about pies would not be complete without the well-known classic cream pie thrown in so many faces by film clowns and other comedians. Eric suggested his mother's recipe. Garnished generously with whipped cream, this pie is absolutely sublime!

SHORT PASTRY CRUST

- Separate the short pastry into two and make two balls.*
- Flour work surface and roll out one ball to make a round pie
- crust 12" (30 cm) in diameter.
- Line the pie plate with the crust.

FILLING

- Preheat the oven to 400°F (200°C).
- In a bowl, mix the sugar and flour.
- Beat the egg white to stiff peaks.
- In a bowl with a wooden spoon, gradually stir the flour and sugar mixture with the cream until the sugar completely dissolves in the cream. It should remain liquid.
- With a spatula, carefully add the egg white to the mixture.
- Pour the mixture into the pie crust.
- Remove the excess pastry around the sides of the pie plate with a knife.
- Bake on the bottom rack of the oven for 10 minutes.
- Lower the temperature to 325°F (160°C) and continue baking on the centre rack for 40 to 50 minutes Baking is complete when a golden, crunchy layer forms on top of the pie.
- Cool on a rack.

WHIPPED CREAM FINISHING

- With a mixer, whip the cream. Add the sugar and vanilla little by little, until the texture is firm.
- Decorate the pie with the whipped cream.

* As this pie uses only half of the short pastry recipe, keep the other half to make another pie, or more nombrils-de-sœurs (recipe on page 146). Wrapped in plastic wrap, the dough will easily last a month in the freezer.

Maple Syrup Nut Crust Pie

Servings: 8 to 10 | **Preparation:** 50 min | **Cooking time:** 45 min
Refrigeration: 1 hr 20 **min** | **Utensils:** 9" (23 cm) round springform pan and a cookie sheet

WALNUT CRUST

- Grind the walnuts, sugar and salt in a food processor until it is the consistency of sand (about 2 minutes).
- Add the cubed butter and pulse for 2 minutes.
- Transfer the mixture to a bowl and add flour. Crumble with your hands.
- Add the egg yolk and water. Mix with your hands until the dough comes together in a ball.
- Wrap the dough in plastic wrap and refrigerate for 20 minutes.
- Preheat the oven to 350°F (180°C).
- Take a quarter of the dough and flatten it with your hands or with a rolling pin on parchment paper to create a rectangle that is about 1/4" (5 mm) thick.
- Cut out 8 diamonds. Slip them onto a parchment-lined cookie sheet.
- Cover the sides of the pan with strips of parchment paper affixed with butter.
- Put the rest of the ball of dough in the centre of the pan and spread it out evenly with your fingers, from the centre to the edges of the pan.
- Cover the dough with parchment paper and place 2 cups (500 ml) of dried peas on top of it (this helps to keep the dough in place while baking).
- Bake the diamonds for a maximum of 10 minutes, making sure they do not burn. Bake the crust for 30 minutes.
- Once baked, take the diamonds out of the oven. Cool at room temperature.
- After 30 minutes, remove the peas and the parchment paper from the crust and continue baking for 15 minutes or until the middle is golden.
- Take out of the oven and let cool for about 30 minutes at room temperature.

INGREDIENTS

WALNUT CRUST

- 1 1/2 cup (375 ml) whole walnuts
- 1/2 cup + 1 tbsp (140 ml) cane sugar
- 1 tsp (5 ml) sea salt
- 1/2 cup (125 ml) unsalted butter, in about 1/4" (5 mm) cubes
- 1 1/2 cup (375 ml) unbleached flour
- 1 egg yolk
- 3 tbsp (45 ml) water

INGREDIENTS

MAPLE SYRUP FILLING

- 1/3 cup (80 ml) corn starch
- 1 cup (250 ml) 35% cream
- 2 cups (500 ml) maple syrup

MAPLE SYRUP FILLING

- In a bowl, dissolve the corn starch into a third of the cream.
- In a pot on medium heat, bring the rest of the cream and the maple syrup to a boil while stirring constantly.
- Mix the boiling maple syrup and cream mixture into the corn starch and cream. Put the whole mixture back into the pot and boil, stirring constantly until it thickens.
- Cool for 10 minutes at room temperature.
- Pour the filling into the nut crust and let rest at room temperature for 2 hours. Place the diamonds on top of the pie.
- Run the blade of a knife between the pan and the pie to turn it out gently.
- Refrigerate for 1 hour before serving.

INGREDIENTS

SWEET PASTRY DOUGH

- 1 Sweet Pastry recipe
  (see page 13)

FILLING

- 1 cup (250 ml) pecans
- 1 cup (250 ml) walnuts
- 1 cup (250 ml) hazelnuts
- 1 1/3 cup (330 ml)
  cane sugar
- 1/3 cup (80 ml) water
- 2/3 cup (165 ml) 35% cream
- 1/4 cup (60 ml)
  unsalted butter

Divine Caramel and Three-Nut Pie

Servings: 8 to 10 | **Preparation:** 30 min | **Cooking time:** 50 min
Utensil: 9" (23 cm) round, fluted tart pan with a removable bottom

This pie is a sensational mouthful with its contrasting textures. Creamy caramel softly caresses the palate, and the light crunch of nuts liberates myriad flavours. The pleasure that follows will take you to seventh heaven!

SWEET PASTRY DOUGH

- Preheat the oven to 350°F (180°C).
- Flour the work surface, roll out the dough with a rolling pin and line the pie plate. Or, place the ball of dough in the centre of the pie plate and spread it out evenly with your fingers from the centre to the edges.
- Cover dough with parchment and place 2 cups (500 ml) of dried peas on top of it (this helps to keep the dough in place while baking).
- On the centre rack, bake the crust through for 30 minutes.
- Remove the peas and parchment paper from the crust and continue to bake for 15 minutes, until the crust is cooked through, or golden.
- Remove the crust from the oven and cool at room temperature for 30 minutes.

FILLING

- Spread out the nuts on a cookie sheet and toast in the oven at 325°F (160°C) for 15 minutes.
- In a small pot, heat the cream.
- In another pot, on medium heat, heat the sugar and water until it caramelizes (see information about caramel on page 160).
- Take the pot off the heat, gradually pour the hot cream into it and mix.
- Add the butter, and mix.
- Mix the nuts into the caramel. Pour into the pie crust.
- Cool and serve with custard or caramel sauce (recipes on pages 156).

Chocolate Pie with Hazelnut Crust

Servings: 8 | Preparation: 40 min | Cooking time: 25 min
Utensil: 9 x 9" (23 x 23 cm) square tart pan with removable bottom

What distinguishes this quickly baked pie is the pairing of a creamy filling and a crispy hazelnut crust. Its texture can be altered to your taste by baking it a little more or a little less. Experiment and taste the difference!

HAZELNUT CRUST

- Grind the ingredients in a food processor, taking care to leave some larger pieces intact.
- Pour the dough into the pan and spread it out with your fingers, from the centre to the edges of the pan.

FILLING

- Preheat the oven to 350°F (180°C).
- Melt the chocolate with the butter with a bain-marie (a large pan filled with hot water).
- Remove from heat, add the sugar and mix well. Let cool.
- Mixing with a wooden spoon, add the eggs, one at a time, and the hazelnut liqueur.
- Pour the mixture on the crust and decorate with whole hazelnuts.
- Bake on the bottom rack for 15 minutes.
- Let cool for 1 hour before serving.
- For added pleasure, serve with raspberry coulis or custard (recipes on page 156).

INGREDIENTS

HAZELNUT CRUST

- 1/4 cup (60 ml) bread crumbs
- 1 cup (250 ml) whole hazelnuts, toasted
- 2 tbsp (30 ml) unsalted butter, melted
- 1 pinch sea salt
- 1 tbsp (15 ml) cane sugar

FILLING

- 1/2 cup (125 ml) dark chocolate, chopped
- 1/2 cup (125 ml) unsalted butter
- 1/3 cup + 1 tbsp (95 ml) cane sugar
- 3 eggs, beaten
- 2 tbsp (30 ml) hazelnut liqueur (like Frangelico)
- 12 whole hazelnuts, toasted

JOSÉE'S RECOMMENDATION

For those who love strong-tasting dark chocolate, I suggest using Michel Cluizel's Mangaro or Los Anconès chocolate. Or, for those who prefer a lighter-tasting dark chocolate, I suggest Cacao Barry's bittersweet chocolate (58% cocoa).

- 1 Sweet Chocolate Pastry recipe (see page 14)

RASPBERRY GANACHE

- 4 1/3 cup (1080 ml) raspberries, fresh or frozen
- 1 1/2 cup (375 ml) dark chocolate, chopped

To highlight the acidic flavour of the raspberries, I strongly suggest using Bittersweet Favorites dark chocolate at 58% cocoa from Cacao Barry. It is a perfect match.

Raspberry Ganache Delight Pie

Servings: 6 to 8 | **Preparation:** 30 min | **Cooking time:** 45 min
Utensil: 8" (20 cm) round tin or 13 1/4 x 4 1/2" (34 x 11 cm) rectangular pan with a removable bottom

SWEET CHOCOLATE PASTRY CRUST

- Preheat the oven to 350°F (180°C).
- Flour the work surface, roll out the dough with a rolling pin and line the pie plate. Or, place the ball of dough in the centre of the pie plate and spread it out evenly with your fingers, from the centre to the edges.
- Cover the dough with parchment paper and place 2 cups (500 ml) of dried peas on top of it (this helps to keep the dough in place while baking).
- Bake in the oven for 30 minutes.
- Remove the peas and the parchment paper from the crust and continue to bake for 10 minutes.
- Remove from the oven and let cool at room temperature for 30 minutes.

RASPBERRY GANACHE

- If you are using frozen raspberries, let them defrost at room temperature.
- Puree the raspberries in the mixer and filter the mixture through a strainer to remove the seeds.
- In a medium-sized pot, heat the raspberry puree on low for 10 minutes.
- Remove the puree from the heat, and mix in the chocolate pieces until they are melted.
- Pour the mixture into the baked crust and let rest at room temperature for 2 hours.
- Decorate with raspberries and mint leaves.

Aunt Annette's Rum-Coconut-Pineapple Pie

Servings: 6 to 8 | **Preparation:** 40 min | **Cooking time:** 40 min
Utensil: 9" (23 cm) round pie plate, Pyrex or ceramic

Eric, my co-author for the book Bread, *often talks about the pies his mother and some of his aunts used to make. This is a modern version of the recipe used by his Aunt Annette, who created this pie for the bishop's home visit. It goes without saying that it was a very special visit! Fresh pineapple was hard to get a hold of at that time. So Eric's aunt used canned pineapple to make this pie. Since things have changed, we ask you to make this recipe with fresh pineapple.*

SHORT PASTRY CRUST

- Separate the short pastry in two and make two balls.*
- Flour the work surface and roll out one ball to make a round pie crust 12" (30 cm) in diameter.
- Line the pie plate with the crust.

FILLING

- Preheat the oven to 425°F (220°C).
- In a bowl, mix the eggs and brown sugar.
- Squeeze the pineapple pulp well between your hands or with the back of a spoon in a strainer to extract all the juice. It is important to extract all the juice from the pulp to get this pie right.
- Add the pressed pulp and the rest of the ingredients to the egg mixture.
- Mix everything, pour it into the pie crust and garnish with the cherries.
- Remove the excess pastry around the sides of the pie plate with a knife.
- Bake on the bottom rack for 10 minutes.
- Lower the temperature to 375°F (190°C) and continue to bake on the centre rack for 30 minutes. Refrigerate for 1 hour. Serve the pie cold.

* As this pie uses only half of the short pastry recipe, keep the other half to make another pie or even nombrils-de-sœurs (recipe on page 146). Wrapped in plastic wrap, the dough will easily last a month in the freezer.

INGREDIENTS

SHORT PASTRY CRUST

- 1 Short Pastry recipe (see page 10)

FILLING

- 3 eggs, beaten
- 1 cup (250 ml) brown sugar
- 2 cups (500 ml) fresh pineapple, lightly crushed in the food processor
- 1 tbsp (15 ml) corn starch
- 2 tsp (10 ml) pure vanilla extract
- 3 tbsp (45 ml) rum
- 1 cup (250 ml) unsweetened, grated coconut
- 15 cherries, pitted

PUFF PASTRY CRUST

- 1 Quick Puff Pastry recipe (see page 16)

FILLING

- 16 to 20 small blue prunes or 10 to 12 red prunes cut in two and pitted
- 1 egg, beaten
- 3 tbsp (45 ml) cane sugar

Plum Pie in Bloom

Servings: 6 to 8 | **Preparation:** 30 min | **Cooking time:** 40 min
Utensil: Cookie sheet

PUFF PASTRY CRUST

- Separate the puff pastry into two equal pieces.
- Flour work surface and roll out one of the pieces of dough to make a round pie crust 13" (33 cm) in diameter.
- Put the rolled-out pastry on a cookie sheet and set aside.

FILLING

- Preheat the oven to 350°F (180°C).
- Dust the pie crust with 1 tablespoon (15 ml) of sugar.
- Pile up the halved plums in a spiral onto the pie crust. Make sure to leave a 2" (5 cm) border.
- Fold the edges of the pastry towards the interior.
- Brush the top of the folded dough with the beaten egg and dust the whole pie with 2 tablespoons (30 ml) of sugar.
- Bake for 30 to 40 minutes, until the crust is golden. Cool and serve.

Gourmet Note

For an even more exquisite experience, serve this pie flambéed with plum liqueur.

*As this recipe only requires half of the quick puff pastry recipe, keep the other half to make another pie, palmier sticks or sesame crackers (recipes on page 146). Wrapped in plastic wrap, the dough will easily last a month in the freezer.

Velvety Peach and Pear Pie

Servings: 6 to 8 | **Preparation:** 40 min | **Cooking time:** 1 hr
Utensil: 9" (23 cm) round pie plate, Pyrex or ceramic

I call this a double-smooth pie. The wonderful marriage of peach and pear is a mouthful of silky sweetness.

COOKIE DOUGH CRUST

- Preheat the oven to 350°F (180°C).
- Place the ball of dough in the centre of the pie plate and spread it out evenly with your fingers, from the centre to the edges.
- Cover the dough with parchment paper and place 2 cups (500 ml) of dried peas on top of it (this helps to keep the dough in place while baking).
- Bake the crust in the oven on the bottom rack for about 10 minutes.
- Take out of the oven. Remove the peas and the parchment paper.
- Pour the fruit mixture into the pie crust.
- Bake in the oven for 50 to 60 minutes, until the crust is golden.
- Cool before serving.

FILLING

- In a bowl, mix all the ingredients well and let rest.

OPTIONAL FINISHING

- Heat the apple jelly without bringing it to a boil.
- Brush the top of the pie as soon as it is out of the oven. This will give it a polished look.

INGREDIENTS

FILLING

- 4 medium peaches, peeled and cut into 3/4" (2 cm) cubes
- 3 large Bartlett pears, peeled and cut into 3/4" (2 cm) cubes
- 1/3 cup (80 ml) cane sugar
- 2 tbsp (30 ml) corn starch

COOKIE DOUGH CRUST

- 1 Cookie Dough recipe (see page 15)

OPTIONAL FINISHING

- 2 tbsp (30 ml) store-bought apple jelly

DOMINIQUE'S ADVICE

Prepare the filling before the pastry. The time it takes to make the pastry will allow the sugar, corn starch and fruit of the filling to blend before baking.

INGREDIENTS

COOKIE DOUGH CRUST

- 1 Cookie Dough recipe (see page 15)

FILLING

- 13 apricots, fresh, cut into two and pitted
- 2 tbsp (30 ml) cane sugar

Henri's Apricot Pie

Servings: 6 to 8 | **Preparation:** 20 min | **Cooking time:** 65 min
Utensil: 9" (23 cm) round pie plate, Pyrex or ceramic

This is the pie that gave me the idea for this book and led to my unforgettable adventure into the world of pie making. Henri Marsand, a close family friend, and in his own way, my mentor, showed me how to make it. Easy to make and extremely tasty, it is a must during apricot season. Take advantage of this time to treat yourself because you can only dream of it through the rest of the year while waiting impatiently for the next harvest. A true favourite!

COOKIE DOUGH CRUST

- Preheat the oven to 350°F (180°C).
- Place the ball of dough in the centre of the pie plate and spread it out evenly with your fingers, from the centre to the edges.
- Cover the dough with parchment paper and place 2 cups (500 ml) of dried peas on top of it (this helps to keep the dough in place while baking).
- Bake the dough in the oven for 10 minutes. Remove the peas and the parchment paper. Set aside.

FILLING

- Place the halved apricots on the pie crust in a spiral. Start from the edges and move toward the centre. Let the fruit halves overlap, with the domed sides facing outward.
- Bake at 350°F (180°C) for 45 minutes, until the crust is golden brown.
- Take out of the oven and dust with sugar.
- Place under the broiler for 1 to 2 minutes to lightly melt the sugar.

Gourmet Note

The taste will be at its best if you use vanilla sugar for the topping (recipe on page 170).

Thin Peach Tart

Servings: 6 to 8 | **Preparation:** 30 min | **Cooking time:** 40 min | **Utensil:** Cookie sheet

I love thin pies! I appreciate their delicious simplicity: very little pastry and a lot of fruit. Each mouthful transforms into a flavour explosion; the taste of the fruit takes centre stage. Throughout the harvests of the seasons, it is easy to create a large variety of thin pies. The most common thin pie is apple, but it is fun to explore numerous other possibilities. So get to it happily!

PUFF PASTRY CRUST

- Separate the puff pastry into two equal pieces.*
- Flour the work surface and roll out one of the pieces of dough to make a 12 x 14" (30 x 35 cm) rectangular pie crust.
- Place the rolled-out pastry on the cookie sheet, dock it with a fork, and set aside.

FILLING

- Preheat the oven to 400°F (200°C).
- Dust half of the sugar on the pie crust.
- Place the pieces of peaches on top of each other in staggered rows.
- Dust with the remainder of the sugar.
- Bake in the oven on the bottom rack for 30 to 40 minutes.
- Serve with raspberry coulis or caramel sauce (recipes on page 156).

SEASONAL VARIETIES

Other than peaches, thin pies can be made with several different fruits, such as apples, pears, nectarines, apricots or cherries, depending on the season.

*As this recipe only requires half of the quick puff pastry recipe, keep the other half to make another pie, palmier sticks or sesame crackers (recipes on page 146). Wrapped in plastic wrap, the dough will easily last a month in the freezer.

INGREDIENTS

PUFF PASTRY CRUST

- 1 Quick Puff Pastry recipe (see page 16)

FILLING

- 1/4 cup (60 ml) cane sugar
- 8 peaches, pitted and cut into eight

DOMINIQUE'S ADVICE

To make this pie, choose only fruits with firm flesh. Fruits with soft flesh, such as strawberries, raspberries, blackberries and melon, lend themselves less to this recipe as they contain too much water.

INGREDIENTS

PUFF PASTRY CRUST

- 1 Quick Puff Pastry recipe (see page 16)

APPLESAUCE

- 4 medium McIntosh apples, cored, peeled and cut into pieces
- 1/4 cup (60 ml) unsalted butter
- 1/4 cup (60 ml) cane sugar

FILLING

- 6 medium Cortland, Empire, Golden or Lobo apples, cored, peeled and sliced thinly
- 1 tbsp (15 ml) unsalted butter, melted
- 1 tbsp (15 ml) cane sugar

DOMINIQUE'S ADVICE

If you use Cortland, Empire, Golden or Lobo apples for the applesauce, crush them while cooking to obtain a smoother consistency.
For a caramel flavour, let the apples stew for an extra 15 minutes.

Applesauce Apple Tart

Servings: 6 to 8 | **Preparation:** 50 min | **Cooking time:** 1 hr
Utensil: 9" (23 cm) round fluted tart pan with a removable bottom

PUFF PASTRY CRUST

- Separate the puff pastry into two equal pieces.*
- Flour the work surface and roll out one of the pieces of dough to make an 11" (28 cm) diameter round pie crust.
- Line the tart pan with the rolled-out pastry, making sure not to stretch the dough.
- Press the dough into the fluting on the sides of the tart pan and dock with a fork.
- Remove excess dough.

APPLESAUCE

- In a large pot, on medium heat, stew the apples with the butter and sugar until they are cooked. The cooking time will vary depending on the apples (allow about 30 minutes).
- Cool at room temperature.

FILLING

- Preheat the oven to 375°F (190°C).
- Spread the applesauce onto the tart crust.
- Place the apples in a spiral, to cover the base of the tart and form a hill in the centre.
- Brush with the melted butter and dust with sugar.
- Bake in the oven on the bottom rack for about 1 hour.
- Serve with custard (recipe on page 156).

*As this recipe only requires half of the quick puff pastry recipe, keep the other half to make another pie, palmier sticks or sesame crackers (recipes on page 146). Wrapped in plastic wrap, the dough will easily last a month in the freezer.

Raspberry Cookie Pie

Servings: 6 to 8 I **Preparation:** 15 min I **Cooking time:** 40 min I **Utensil:** Cookie sheet

A favourite! This pie is a succulent example of what can be created when we have fun with experimentation and bake outside the box! A true pleasure, this large cookie bursting with fresh raspberries is a unanimous hit. Created by my friend, Diane, this pie is, hands down, her favourite. Those who are apt at baking cookies will be delighted.

COOKIE DOUGH CRUST
- Preheat the oven to 350°F (180°C).
- Line the cookie sheet with parchment paper.
- Place the ball of dough in the centre of the cookie sheet and spread it out evenly, from the centre toward the exterior, to make an oval shape about 12 x 6" (30 x 15 cm) in size.
- Blind bake in the oven for 10 minutes.
- Brush the top of the pastry with half a beaten egg, making sure to go to the edges.
- Bake in the oven for an extra 3 minutes.

FILLING
- Garnish the baked cookie pastry with raspberries, leaving a border of about 1" (2.5 cm) all around ungarnished.
- Dust sugar on the raspberries and the border.
- Bake in the oven for 25 to 30 minutes, until the crust is golden brown.

BLUEBERRY OR GRAPE VARIATION
- Replace the raspberries with blueberries or grapes. After pre-baking, push them into the pastry and bake again.
- Brush with hot apple jelly after taking it out of the oven.

INGREDIENTS

COOKIE DOUGH CRUST
- 1 Cookie Dough recipe (see page 15)
- 1 egg, beaten

FILLING
- 2 cups (500 ml) fresh raspberries
- 2 tbsp (30 ml) cane sugar

INGREDIENTS

BUNDLE PASTRY CRUST

- 1 cup (250 ml) unbleached flour
- 1/8 tsp (0.5 ml) baking powder
- 1/4 tsp (1 ml) sea salt
- 1/4 cup (60 ml) unsalted butter, soft
- 1 egg, beaten

FILLING

- 3 large Cortland, Empire, Golden or Lobo apples, cored, peeled and diced
- 3/4 cup (175 ml) cranberries, fresh or frozen
- 1/4 cup + 1 tbsp (75 ml) cane sugar
- 1 1/2 tbsp (25 ml) unbleached flour
- 1 pinch sea salt
- 1 egg, beaten
- 1 cup (250 ml) 14% sour cream
- 1 tsp (5 ml) pure vanilla extract

Apple Cranberry Pie

Servings: 8 | Preparation: 30 min | Cooking time: 50 min | Utensil: Cookie sheet

BUNDLE PASTRY CRUST

- In a large bowl, sift together the flour and baking powder.
- Add the salt and butter. Crumble everything together.
- Add the egg and mix to form a ball.
- Wrap with plastic wrap and refrigerate for 30 minutes.
- On a floured work surface, roll out the dough to a 16" (40 cm) diameter ball.
- Line a cookie sheet with parchment paper and spread out the dough.
- Set aside.

FILLING

- Preheat the oven to 400°F (200°C).
- Pare the fruit in order to spread it out quickly.
- In a large bowl, mix 1/4 cup (60 ml) of sugar and all the ingredients, except the apples and cranberries.
- Pour the mixture onto the pastry, leaving an ungarnished edge of 2" (5 cm).
- Ring the mixture with the fruit to hold it in place. Then cover the rest of the bottom.
- Fold the excess pastry over, brush the top with water and dust it with 1 tablespoon (15 ml) of sugar.
- Bake on the centre rack for 10 minutes.
- Lower the temperature to 350°F (180°C) and continue to bake for 40 minutes or until the filling sets.
- Cool on a rack.
- Serve with caramel sauce (recipe on page 156).

Lightly Scented Orange Cheese Pie

Servings: 8 to 10 | **Preparation:** 20 min | **Cooking time:** 40 min | **Utensil:** 9" (23 cm) round springform pan

SWEET PASTRY CRUMB CRUST (MAKE THE NIGHT BEFORE)

- In a bowl, mix the butter and crumbs by hand until the dough comes together.
- Line the bottom of the pan with the dough, making sure to press the crumbs well (do not go up the sides).

ORANGE SCENTED CREAM CHEESE

- Preheat the oven to 350°F (180°C).
- In a mixer, beat the cream cheese until smooth.
- Add the sugar, zest, mascarpone cheese and beaten eggs. Mix well.
- Spread out the mixture on the crust.
- Bake in the oven for about 40 minutes or until the top starts to brown around the pan.
- Take out of the oven. Let rest 5 minutes and then remove the springform from around the pie.
- Refrigerate, then decorate with fresh fruit or serve with raspberry coulis (recipe on page 156).

INGREDIENTS

SWEET PASTRY CRUMB CRUST

- 1/4 cup (60 ml) unsalted butter, melted
- 2 cups (500 ml) sweet pastry crumbs (recipe on page 14)

LIGHTLY SCENTED ORANGE CREAM CHEESE

- 1 1/2 cups (375 ml) cream cheese (like Philadelphia), room temperature
- 1/2 cup (125 ml) cane sugar
- Zest of 1 orange
- 2 1/2 cups (625 ml) mascarpone cheese
- 2 eggs, beaten

DOMINIQUE'S ADVICE

When you take this pie out of the oven, slide a thin knife between the pie and the pan. Wait 5 minutes before removing the springform. This prevents the sides from sticking and the middle from falling.

INGREDIENTS

- 2 1/2 cups (625 ml) fresh cherries, whole, washed and hulled to cover the bottom of the pie plate
- 4 medium eggs, beaten
- 1/2 cup (125 ml) cane sugar
- 1/3 cup + 2 tbsp (110 ml) unbleached flour
- 1 pinch sea salt
- 1/3 cup (80 ml) unsalted butter, melted
- 1 cup (250 ml) milk, hot

OPTIONAL FINISHING

- 2 tbsp (30 ml) cane sugar

Clafoutis

Servings: 6 to 8 | **Preparation:** 20 min | **Cooking time:** 40 min
Utensil: 9" (23 cm) round pie plate, Pyrex or ceramic

This speciality from the Limousin region in France evokes good memories of my adolescence. I would spend time with family friends in Avignon, where we would pick cherries to make clafoutis. To my amazement, my hosts made it with the pits in the cherries! They explained that the pits were necessary for the flavour and that clafoutis without pits isn't true clafoutis. It stayed with me. My children sometimes ask me to remove the pits when I make this dessert at home, and from time to time, I let them convince me. And even if the result is delicious, I can't help thinking that clafoutis without the pits isn't the real deal.

- Preheat the oven to 350°F (180°C). Butter the pie plate.
- Arrange the cherries on the bottom of the pie plate, making sure to cover the entire surface.
- Mix the eggs gently with a whisk, adding the sugar bit by bit.
- Gradually add the flour and salt, still mixing with a whisk.
- Add the melted butter and milk. Mix until the consistency is smooth.
- Pour the mixture over the cherries and bake for 30 to 40 minutes.
- To ensure it is fully baked, insert a toothpick into the clafoutis. If it comes out clean, it is ready.

OPTIONAL FINISHING

- Once the clafoutis is cooked, dust with sugar and place under the broiler for 1 to 2 minutes.
- Cool at room temperature and serve.

Gourmet Note

This will taste best if you use vanilla sugar for the topping (recipe on page 169).

Lady Marmalade Pie

Servings: 8 | **Preparation:** 1 hr | **Cooking time:** 1 hr
Utensil: 9" (23 cm) shallow round pie plate, Pyrex or ceramic

SHORT PASTRY CRUST

- Separate the short pastry in two and make two balls.
- Flour the work surface and roll out each ball into a round pie crust, 11" (28 cm) in diameter.
- Line the pie plate with the first crust.
- Fold the second crust in two, and make cuts into it with a knife. Set aside.

FILLING

- Preheat the oven to 400°F (200°C).
- Section the oranges. (method on page 166).
- Peel the lime and cut it into thin slices.
- Thinly slice the unpeeled lemon (it is important that the skin be thin).
- Mix the citrus with 1 cup (250 ml) of sugar, the eggs and the vanilla.
- Pour it into the pie crust and set aside.
- Brush the edges of the pastry with water. Cover with the other rolled-out dough. Cut off the excess pastry with a knife.
- Scallop the edges by pinching the pastry with your fingers.
- Brush the top of the pie with water and dust with 2 tablespoons (30 ml) of sugar.
- Bake on the bottom rack of the oven for 15 minutes.
- Lower the temperature of the oven to 350°F (180°C). Continue to bake on the centre rack for 30 minutes or until the crust is golden brown.
- Cool before serving.

INGREDIENTS

SHORT PASTRY CRUST

- 1 Short Pastry recipe (see page 10)

FILLING

- 2 navel oranges without seeds
- 1 lime
- 1 Meyer lemon or 1 thin-skinned lemon
- 1 cup + 2 tbsp (280 ml) cane sugar
- 4 eggs, beaten
- 2 tsp (10 ml) pure vanilla extract

INGREDIENTS

CRÊPE BATTER

- 1/3 cup (80 ml) unbleached flour
- 1/2 tsp (2.5 ml) baking powder
- 1 tbsp (15 ml) cane sugar
- 1 pinch sea salt
- 1 pinch ground nutmeg
- 4 eggs, lightly beaten
- 1 cup (250 ml) milk
- 2 tbsp (30 ml) unsalted butter, melted
- 1 tbsp (15 ml) pure vanilla extract

FILLING

- 1 tbsp (15 ml) unsalted butter
- 1/3 cup + 1 tbsp (95 ml) cane sugar
- 4 Bosc or Bartlett pears, cored, peeled and quartered
- 1/2 tsp (2.5 ml) ground nutmeg

OPTIONAL FINISHING

- 1 tbsp (15 ml) icing sugar

Pear and Nutmeg Crêpe Pie

Servings: 6 to 8 | **Preparation:** 30 min | **Cooking time:** 30 min
Utensil: 9" (23 cm) cast-iron pan is preferable, or any oven-safe pan

CRÊPE BATTER

- In a bowl, mix the flour, baking powder, sugar, salt and nutmeg.
- In a different bowl, whisk the eggs, milk, butter and vanilla.
- Add the egg mixture to the flour mixture. Beat until the batter is smooth, without lumps.
- Let rest in the fridge for 30 minutes.

FILLING

- Preheat the oven to 400°F (200°C).
- Butter the bottom and the sides of the pan.
- Dust the bottom of the pan with 1/3 cup (80 ml) of sugar.
- Arrange the pieces of pears on the bottom of the pan.
- Dust with the rest of the sugar and the ground nutmeg.
- Cook on the stove on medium heat for 5 minutes.
- Leaving the pan on the heat, delicately add the crêpe batter onto the pears. It will begin to cook and bubble on the sides.
- Bake in the oven for about 15 minutes.
- Reduce the temperature of the oven to 350°F (180°C) and continue to bake for 15 minutes, or until the centre is cooked.
- The pie is ready when a toothpick inserted into the dough comes out clean.

OPTIONAL FINISHING

- Dust with icing sugar and serve.
- For a complete delight, serve the pie freshly baked, still in the pan, accompanied by crème fraîche or custard (recipe on page 156).

Grape Pie in a Pan

Servings: 6 to 8 | **Preparation:** 20 min | **Cooking time:** 45 min
Refrigeration: 1 hr **Utensil:** 9" (23 cm) cast-iron pan is preferred

Here is a pie that draws inspiration from the dough of the Cannelés Bordelais. Its crunchy crust, formed while baking, and its soft filling, like a caramelized flan covered with juicy grapes, make an original dessert.

PREPARATION

- In a pot, heat the milk, vanilla and 1/4 cup (60 ml) butter. Bring to a boil.
- Whisk the flour and sugar. Then, add the eggs and the rum to the mixture.
- Pour the scalding milk into the mixture.
- Gently mix to get a smooth crêpe-like batter.
- Cool in the refrigerator for 1 hour.
- Preheat the oven to 400°F (200°C).
- In a very hot pan, melt 1 tablespoon (15 ml) of butter.
- Gradually pour the smooth batter into the pan and cook for 1 minute.
- Cover the whole surface of the batter with grapes.
- Continue to bake in the oven on the bottom rack for 45 to 55 minutes.
- Serve the pie hot, in the pan.
- This pie is delightful served freshly baked, still in the pan, accompanied by crème fraîche or custard (recipe on page 156).

PINEAPPLE VARIATION

Replace grapes with pieces of fresh pineapple.

INGREDIENTS

- 1 cup (250 ml) milk
- 1 tsp (5 ml) pure vanilla extract
- 1/4 cup + 1 tbsp (75 ml) unsalted butter
- 1/4 cup (60 ml) unbleached flour
- 1/2 cup + 1 tbsp (140 ml) icing sugar
- 2 eggs, beaten
- 1 tbsp (15 ml) rum or brandy
- 2 cups (500 ml) white or red seedless grapes

DOMINIQUE'S ADVICE

To get this pie right, the pan must be very hot before the butter is melted. For this reason, we recommend a cast-iron pan. The batter should simmer on contact with the pan. Also, with a cast-iron pan the pie will continue to bake when taken out of the oven, which keeps it hot and delicious.

INGREDIENTS

- 1 Quick Puff Pastry recipe (see page 16)

FILLING

- 2 tbsp (30 ml) unsalted butter, room temperature
- 1/3 cup + 1 tbsp (95 ml) cane sugar
- 10 to 12 medium Cortland, Empire, Golden or Lobo apples, cored, peeled and cut in two

---

DOMINIQUE'S ADVICE

It is important not to let the caramel cook too long as it will turn bitter. For more information on caramel, see page 160.

The texture of the tart will vary if you use different kinds of apples other than Cortland, Empire, Golden or Lobo. More importantly, it could lead to a variation in cooking time. If the pastry is too inflated when it is taken out of the oven, put a plate on top and apply light pressure. Remove the plate. Turn out the pie 30 to 45 minutes later.

Tempting Tart Tatin

Servings: 6 | **Preparation:** 45 min | **Cooking time:** 3 hrs 15 min
Utensil: 10" (25 cm) diameter oven-safe pan

PUFF PASTRY CRUST

- Separate the puff pastry into four equal pieces.*
- Flour the work surface, roll out one of the pieces of dough to form a round pie crust 11" (28 cm) in diameter. Set aside.

FILLING

- Preheat the oven to 325^{0}F (160^{0}C).
- Cook the butter and the sugar in a pan on medium-high heat, until they turn into caramel.
- Let the caramel cool. Place the halved apples standing up, very tight against each other, with the domed sides against the hollow ones.
- Bake in the oven for 2 hours and 30 minutes.
- Remove from the oven. Raise the temperature to 400^{0}F (200^{0}C).
- Cover the apples with the pastry and fold the edges toward the inside of the pan.
- Bake again for 30 to 45 minutes, until the pastry is baked through.
- Cool for 30 to 45 minutes at room temperature.
- Place a serving dish as big as the pan on top of it and quickly turn it over to turn the tart out.
- Serve as is or with crème fraîche.

* As this tart only requires a quarter of the quick puff pastry recipe, keep the other three pieces to make other pies, palmier sticks or sesame crackers (recipes on page 146). Wrapped in plastic wrap, the dough will easily last a month in the freezer.

Lemon Meringue Pie

Servings: 6 to 8 | **Preparation:** 50 min | **Cooking time:** 45 min
Utensil: 8" (20 cm) round fluted tart pan with a removable bottom

SWEET PASTRY CRUST

- Preheat the oven to 350°F (180°C).
- Flour the work surface, roll out the dough with a rolling pin and line the pie plate. Or, place the ball of dough in the centre of the pie plate and spread it out evenly with your fingers, from the centre to the edges.
- Cover dough with parchment paper and place 2 cups (500 ml) of dried peas on top of it (this helps to keep the dough in place while baking).
- Bake the pie crust in the oven for 30 minutes.
- Remove the peas and the parchment paper from the crust and continue to bake for 15 minutes, until the crust is cooked through or golden.
- Take it out of the oven and cool at room temperature for 30 minutes.

LEMON CREAM

- In a pot, bring the lemon juice to a boil.
- Let the gelatin bloom in 1 tablespoon (15 ml) of cold water for 5 minutes.
- Whisk the egg yolks and sugar until the mixture is frothy.
- Add the lemon juice and mix well.
- Put the mixture back into the pot and cook on medium-high heat until it comes to a boil, stirring constantly with a whisk.
- Stop cooking. Add the gelatin and butter and emulsify everything with a hand-held blender.
- Pour the mixture onto the baked pie crust and cool in the refrigerator.

INGREDIENTS

SWEET PASTRY CRUST

- 1 Sweet Pastry recipe (see page 13)

LEMON CREAM

- 1 cup (250 ml) lemon juice, freshly squeezed
- 1/2 package (1 tsp or 5 ml) gelatin
- 4 egg yolks
- 1/2 cup (125 ml) cane sugar
- 1/2 cup (125 ml) unsalted butter

DOMINIQUE'S ADVICE

The egg-white mixture and sugar should not boil as they won't rise when you beat them with a mixer. It is ideal to eat a lemon meringue pie the same day it is made. Meringue has a tendency to melt and leave water on the pie after a few hours. You could also prepare the pie with the lemon cream in advance (it will keep a few days in the fridge) and make the meringue before serving.

SWISS MERINGUE

- 4 egg whites
- 1/2 cup (125 ml) cane sugar

SWISS MERINGUE

- Boil water in a pot for the base of a bain-marie (or double boiler).
- Put the egg whites and sugar into a smaller container and lower it into the pot so it is immersed halfway into the water. Whisk the ingredients constantly.
- When the mixture becomes consistent and hot to touch, remove from heat. It should not boil.
- With a mixer, beat the hot mixture until firm peaks form.
- Cover the lemon cream entirely with the hot meringue mixture.
- Place under the broiler for about 2 minutes, watching the meringue so it doesn't burn (it can happen quickly).
- Serve with raspberry coulis (recipe on page 156).

APPLE FILLING

- 8 apples (or as many as necessary), preferably Cortland, Empire, Golden or Lobo, cored, peeled and cut into eight
- 2 tbsp (30 ml) cane sugar

MY GRANDMOTHER'S CRISP

- 1/2 cup (125 ml) unsalted butter, soft
- 1 cup (250 ml) brown sugar
- 1 cup + 3 tbsp (295 ml) unbleached flour

My Grandmother's Apple Crisp

Servings: 6 to 8 | **Preparation:** 15 min | **Cooking time:** 40 min
Utensil: 9" (23 cm) round deep-dish; 8 x 8" (20 cm x 20 cm) square or 8 x 12" (20 x 30 cm) rectangular pan

The selection of recipes for this book was finished. I was at home on a sunny day off. I was in the garden with my mother, talking about the book and other things, when my daughter said she was hungry and asked me to make her a pie. It was hot, and I honestly did not want to be cooped up in the house on such a nice day! My mother gave me the idea of making a crisp. What a great idea! Fifteen minutes and it was in the oven! I grew up with seasonal fruit crisps made by my mom and grandmother. I realized that I had forgotten this very close familial pie for this book. By the next day, I had convinced the whole team to add it for the sake of my childhood memories—and those of many others, I'm sure.

APPLE FILLING

- Spread out the apples in the bottom of the pan to cover the entire surface.
- Dust with sugar.

MY GRANDMOTHER'S CRISP

- Preheat the oven to 350°F (180°C).
- With your hands, mix the butter and brown sugar.
- Add the flour. Mix with a wooden spoon. It should have lumps.
- Pour the mixture over the fruit.
- Bake for 30 to 40 minutes, until the fruit is cooked and the crisp is golden brown.
- Serve with a dollop of crème fraîche or a scoop of vanilla ice cream.

SEASONAL VARIETIES

Besides apples, this crisp is tasty with every seasonal fruit: strawberries, raspberries, blueberries, peaches, apricots, pears, etc. Of course, you can also mix fruits depending on your taste.

FRESH PIES

Anyone who knows me will attest that I'm a bit of a "hippie." I have a bias for fresh, seasonal products, natural foods and healthy ingredients. I care about my health and it is certainly reflected in my approach to cooking. And if Dominique and I understand each other so well, it's because of more than our mutual love of food—he also shares this healthy perspective with me. All the pies in this section experiment with various "hippie" forms, with a few gourmet contradictions as a bonus! Because, I confess, there are a few. You will find such discrepancies as pastry cream, caramel and almond cream in this universe of pie crusts made from tofu or nuts and filling created from seasonal fruit, ricotta and sesame. In short, I hope this is a

Strawberry and Almond Pie on a Soft French Toast Crust

Servings: 8 to 10 | **Preparation:** 30 min | **Cooking time:** 1 hr
Utensil: 9" (23 cm) round pie plate, Pyrex or ceramic

FRENCH TOAST CRUST

- Preheat the oven to 350°F (180°C).
- In a bowl, beat together the hot milk, sugar and eggs.
- Let the slices of bread soak in the egg mixture.
- Butter the pie plate and line the bottom with the five slices of egg-soaked bread.
- Bake in the oven for 25 minutes.

ALMOND CREAM

- In a bowl with a spatula, cream the butter and sugar to obtain a light yellow cream. Add the beaten egg.
- Add the rest of the ingredients and mix well. Pour the mixture onto the cooked French toast bottom and continue to bake in the oven for 35 minutes.

STRAWBERRY FILLING

- Spread the top of the pie with jam.
- Garnish with strawberries.

OPTIONAL FINISHING

With a sieve, dust the pie with icing sugar, or cover it with a hot apple jelly or honey topping to give it a nice sheen (recipe on page 169).

Gourmet Note

Serve this pie warm with whipped cream, strawberry coulis or custard (recipes on page 156).

INGREDIENTS

FRENCH TOAST CRUST

- 1 cup (250 ml) hot milk
- 1/4 cup (60 ml) maple or cane sugar
- 2 eggs
- 5 thin slices of white bread or day-old country loaf
- 2 tsp (10 ml) unsalted butter

ALMOND CREAM

- 1/2 cup (125 ml) unsalted butter, soft
- 1/3 cup (80 ml) cane sugar
- 1 egg, beaten
- 1/4 cup (60 ml) unbleached flour
- 1 1/4 cups (310 ml) almond powder
- 1/3 cup (80 ml) pecans, toasted and ground

STRAWBERRY FILLING

- 3 tbsp (45 ml) strawberry jam
- 2 cups (500 ml) fresh strawberries

INGREDIENTS

ALMOND AND
OATMEAL CRUST

- 1 cup (250 ml) whole almonds
- 1 cup (250 ml) oatmeal
- 1/4 tsp (1 ml) sea salt
- 2 tbsp (30 ml) canola oil
- 1/4 cup (60 ml) water
- 1/4 cup (60 ml) maple syrup

FILLING

- 2 tbsp (30 ml) blueberry jam
- 2 cups (500 ml) fresh blueberries

Blueberry Pie on a Crunchy Almond Crust

Servings: 6 to 8 | **Preparation:** 30 min | **Cooking time:** 40 min | **Utensil:** Cookie sheet

ALMOND AND OATMEAL CRUST

- Preheat the oven to 300°F (150°C).
- Grind the almonds in a food processor until they are the size of oatmeal.
- Mix the oatmeal, almonds and salt.
- With a fork, beat the oil, water and maple syrup. Add this to the dry mixture.
- Let it rest for 10 minutes so that the oatmeal can soak up the liquid. Form a ball with your hands.
- Line a cookie sheet with parchment paper and spread out the dough with your fingers to make an 8" (20 cm) diameter crust.
- Bake the crust in the centre of the oven for 30 to 40 minutes, until it is golden.
- Cool at room temperature.

FILLING

- Heat the jam and mix with the blueberries.
- Cover the crust with the blueberry filling right before serving.
- To heighten your pleasure, serve the pie with frozen yogurt or sorbet.

Jardinière Fruit Tart

Servings: 6 to 8 I **Preparation:** 35 min I **Cooking time:** 45 min
Refrigeration: 1 hr 30 min I **Utensil:** 9" (23 cm) round tart pan with removable bottom

SWEET PASTRY CRUST

- Preheat the oven to 350°F (180°C).
- Flour the work surface, roll out the dough with a rolling pin and line the pie plate. Or, place the ball of dough in the centre of the pie plate and spread it out evenly with your fingers, from the centre to the edges.
- Cover the dough with parchment paper. Place 2 cups (500 ml) of dried peas on top of it (this helps to keep the dough in place while baking).
- Bake the pie crust in the oven for 30 minutes.
- Remove the peas and the parchment paper. Continue to bake for 15 minutes or until the crust is baked through and golden.
- Cool at room temperature for about 30 minutes.

PASTRY CREAM

- Split the halved vanilla pod in half lengthwise with a knife and remove the seeds with the tip of a knife.
- In a pot, bring the milk, vanilla pod and seeds to a boil.
- Once boiling, remove the pod.
- In a bowl, mix the egg yolks with the sugar and corn starch.
- Gradually whisk in the hot milk.
- Put the whole mixture back into the pot and cook it, whisking until it comes to a boil. Remove from heat and add butter.
- Cool for 1 hour and 30 minutes in the refrigerator.

FILLING

- Cut the fruit to your liking.
- Spread the pastry cream on the pie crust and garnish with the fruit.

OPTIONAL TOPPING

- Without bringing to a boil, heat the apple jelly and brush the jardinière to make the fruit shine.
- Serve with custard or raspberry coulis (recipes on page 156).

Gourmet Note

Afterwards, dry the vanilla pod and use it to make vanilla sugar (recipe on page 170).

INGREDIENTS

SWEET PASTRY CRUST

- 1 Sweet Pastry recipe (see page 13)

PASTRY CREAM

- 1/2 vanilla pod
- 5 egg yolks
- 1/2 cup (125 ml) cane sugar
- 1/4 cup (60 ml) corn starch
- 1 cup (250 ml) milk
- 1 tbsp (15 ml) unsalted butter

FILLING

- Your choice of fresh fruit

OPTIONAL FINISHING

- 1/4 cup (60 ml) store-bought apple jelly

- 1 1/4 cups (310 ml) whole walnuts
- 1 cup (250 ml) oatmeal
- 1/4 tsp (1 ml) sea salt
- 2 tbsp (30 ml) nut oil
- 1/4 cup (60 ml) water
- 1/4 cup (60 ml) honey

FILLING

- 1/2 cup (125 ml) fresh cheese (like Old Style Cottage Cheese by Liberty)
- 2 tbsp (30 ml) honey
- 3 cups (750 ml) fresh raspberries

Cream Cheese Pie with Honey and Raspberries

Servings: 6 to 8 | **Preparation:** 30 min | **Cooking time:** 50 min | **Utensil:** Cookie sheet

WALNUT AND OATMEAL CRUST

- Preheat the oven to 300°F (150°C).
- Grind the walnuts in a food processor until they are the size of the oatmeal.
- Mix the oatmeal with the ground nuts and salt.
- With a fork, whisk the oil, water and honey. Add this to the dry mixture.
- Let rest for 10 minutes so the oatmeal can soak up the liquid. Make a ball with your hands.
- Line a cookie sheet with parchment paper and spread out the dough with your fingers to make an 8" (20 cm) diameter crust.
- Bake the crust in the centre of the oven for 40 to 50 minutes, until it is golden.
- Cool at room temperature.

FILLING

- Mix the cottage cheese with the honey.
- To ensure the crust remains crunchy, cover it with the cheese and honey mixture just before serving. Garnish with the raspberries.
- Serve with raspberry coulis (recipe on page 156)...naturally!

Intoxicating Red Wine Pear Tart

Servings: 6 to 8 | **Preparation:** 30 min | **Cooking time:** 45 min | **Refrigeration:** 1 hr 30 min
Macerating the pears: At least 24 hrs | **Utensil:** 14 x 5" (36 x 13 cm) rectangular pan
or 8" (20 cm) round pie plate with a removable bottom

RED WINE PEARS

- Peel the pears, cut them in half and remove the core with a melon baller. Place them in an airtight container.
- Put the rest of the ingredients in a pot and bring to a boil.
- Pour the boiling wine syrup onto the pears, cover and let macerate in the refrigerator for 24 to 48 hours.

SHORTBREAD PASTRY CRUST

- Preheat the oven to 350°F (180°C).
- Spread the dough with your fingers to completely cover the bottom of the pan.
- Bake the shortbread pastry crust in the oven for 30 minutes.
- Take it out the oven and cool for about 30 minutes at room temperature.

PASTRY CREAM

- Split the halved vanilla pod lengthwise in two with a knife and remove the seeds with the tip of the knife.
- In a pot, bring the milk, vanilla pod and seeds to a boil.
- When everything is boiling, remove the pod.
- In a bowl, mix the egg yolks, sugar and corn starch.
- Gradually whisk in the hot milk.
- Cook the mixture while whisking until it begins to boil.
- Take off the heat and add the butter.
- Let cool for 1 hour and 30 minutes in the fridge.

ASSEMBLY

- Spread the pastry cream on the pie crust, leaving a 3/8" (1 cm) ungarnished border all around. Keeping the syrup, drain the pears. Place them on a paper towel. Slice and arrange them to your liking on the pastry cream.

INGREDIENTS

RED WINE PEARS

- 5 medium, ripe Bartlett pears
- 1 1/2 cups (375 ml) cane sugar
- 1 cup (250 ml) water
- 2 cinnamon sticks
- 3 pieces star anise
- 1 cup (250 ml) red wine

SHORTBREAD PASTRY CRUST

- 1 Shortbread Pastry recipe (see page 15)

PASTRY CREAM

- 1/2 vanilla pod
- 1 cup (250 ml) milk
- 5 egg yolks
- 1/2 cup (125 ml) cane sugar
- 1/4 cup (60 ml) corn starch
- 1 tbsp (15 ml) unsalted butter

DOMINIQUE'S ADVICE

It is important to let the pears macerate in the fridge for at least 24 hours so they are infused with the flavours of the wine mixture. For this recipe, take advantage of a wine rich in colour and depth like a cabernet, merlot or syrah to give a nice, deep colour to the pears.

INGREDIENTS

CHOCOLATE WINE SAUCE

- 3 cups (750 ml) wine syrup (the syrup used to macerate the pears)
- 1/2 cup (125 ml) 70% cocoa chocolate, chopped

OPTIONAL FINISHING CHOCOLATE WINE SAUCE

- In a pan, reduce the maceration syrup in half by boiling on high heat for 10 minutes.
- Put the chocolate in a large double boiler. Pour in the hot syrup reduction, little by little, and mix with a wooden spoon.

JOSÉE'S RECOMMENDATION

For a really out-of-the-ordinary taste experience, make the chocolate wine sauce with Guanaja chocolate from Valrhona.

INGREDIENTS

TOFU AND TWO-SESAME CRUST

- 1 cup + 2 tbsp (280 ml) unbleached flour
- 1 pinch baking powder
- 1 1/3 cups (330 ml) firm tofu, crumbled
- 1/3 cup (80 ml) cane sugar
- 1 egg, beaten
- 2 tsp (10 ml) sesame oil
- 1 tbsp (15 ml) white sesame seeds
- 1 tbsp (15 ml) black sesame seeds

RICOTTA AND LIME FILLING

- 1 container (475 g) ricotta
- 1/4 cup (60 ml) honey
- 2 eggs, beaten
- Zest of 2 or 3 limes, finely grated

DOMINIQUE'S ADVICE

It is important to remove only the green part of the skin of the lime. If the white part of the rind is included in the zest, it makes for a bitter pie.

Min's Korean Ricotta and Lime Pie

Servings: 6 to 8 | Preparation: 30 min | Cooking time: 1 hr 15 min
Utensil: 9" (23 cm) round pie plate with a removable bottom

We asked Min, who helped us put this book together, to develop a pie with the flavours of her home country of South Korea. Her fresh offering is marked by its amazing tofu and sesame crust. Korean women eat tofu regularly as it is non-fattening and helps maintain weight. Min explained to us that black sesame was known to contribute to healthy hair. So, you can treat yourself guilt-free!

TOFU AND TWO-SESAME CRUST

- Preheat the oven to 350°F (180°C).
- Sift the baking powder with the flour.
- Mix all the crust ingredients by hand and make a ball.
- Place the ball of dough in the centre of the pie plate and spread it out evenly with your fingers, from the centre to the edges.
- Cover the dough with parchment paper. Place 2 cups (500 ml) of dried peas on top of it (this helps to keep the dough in place while baking).
- Bake the pie crust in the oven for 30 minutes.
- Remove the peas and the parchment paper. Continue to bake for 15 minutes, until the crust is golden brown.
- Take it out the oven and cool for about 30 minutes at room temperature.

RICOTTA AND LIME FILLING

- Mix together the ricotta and honey until creamy.
- Add the beaten eggs and lime zest.
- Fill the crust with the mixture.
- Bake in the oven for about 30 minutes at 350°F (180°C).
- Cool and serve with raspberry coulis.

Gourmet Note

To enhance this exquisite and exotic pie even more, garnish it with candied limes (recipe on page 149). A pleasure for the eyes as well as the palate!

Mango and Apricot Spelt Pancake Pie

Servings: 8 | Preparation: 1 hr | Cooking time: 45 min | Refrigeration: 40 min
Utensil: 9" (23 cm) round pie plate, Pyrex or ceramic, or an 8 x 8" (20 x 20 cm) square pan

MANGO AND APRICOT GELÉE

- In a pot, mix the apricot nectar and agar agar. Bring to a boil.
- Turn down the heat and simmer gently for 5 to 10 minutes, or until the flakes are completely dissolved.
- Add the mango cubes and mix.
- Line the square pan with plastic wrap and pour in the mixture.
- Refrigerate for 40 minutes to set the gelée.

WHITE CHOCOLATE GANACHE

- Without bringing to a boil, heat the cream.
- In a bowl, carefully pour the hot cream onto the white chocolate and mix with a wooden spoon until it is completely melted.
- Mix with a hand-held blender for 30 minutes until the ganache is homogeneous. Set aside.

SPELT PANCAKE CRUST

- Preheat the oven to 350°F (180°C) and butter the pie plate.
- In a bowl, mix all the ingredients with a spatula until the dough is homogeneous.
- Pour the mixture into the buttered pie plate.
- Bake for 30 to 35 minutes, until the dough is golden brown.
- Turn out the spelt pancake onto a rack to cool.

ASSEMBLY

- Place the pancake on a serving dish.
- Spread the top of the pancake with the white chocolate ganache.
- Turn out the gelée and cut into 3/4" (1.5 cm) cubes.
- Place the cubes on the pancake covered in ganache.

INGREDIENTS

MANGO AND APRICOT GELÉE

- 2 cups (500 ml) thick apricot nectar
- 10 1/2 oz (300 g) mangoes, cubed into about 3/8" (6 mm) pieces (2 mangoes)
- 2 tbsp (30 ml) agar agar flakes (sold in health-food stores)

WHITE CHOCOLATE GANACHE

- 3 tbsp (45 ml) 35% cream
- 2/3 cup (165 ml) white chocolate, chopped

SPELT PANCAKE CRUST

- 2 tbsp (30 ml) honey
- 1 1/2 cup (375 ml) spelt flour
- 2 tsp (10 ml) baking powder
- 1 cup (250 ml) milk
- 1 egg, beaten

INGREDIENTS

MILK CHOCOLATE AND PEANUT CRUST

- 1 1/2 cups (375 ml) milk chocolate, chopped
- 3/4 cup (175 ml) unsalted peanuts

DARK CHOCOLATE TOFU CREAM

- 2 1/2 cups (625 ml) soft tofu
- 1/2 cup (125 ml) sweetened condensed milk
- 1 cup (250 ml) dark chocolate, chopped

VARIATION YOGURT AND MILK CHOCOLATE

- 1 1/2 cups (375 ml) thick plain yogurt (10%)
- 1 1/2 cups (375 ml) milk chocolate, chopped

JOSÉE'S RECOMMENDATION

For a contrast between the milk chocolate crust and the dark chocolate tofu cream, I suggest using Guanaja 70% cocoa from Valrhona.

Dark Chocolate Tofu Pie on a Peanut Chocolate Crust

Servings: 6 to 8 | **Preparation:** 30 min | **Cooking time:** none | **Refrigeration:** 4 hrs
Utensil: 9" (23 cm) round pie plate, Pyrex or ceramic

MILK CHOCOLATE AND PEANUT CRUST

- In a food processor, grind the chocolate and peanuts until you obtain dough. Make a ball of dough with your hands.
- Spread out the dough with your fingers in the pie plate right up to the top of the sides and refrigerate for 30 minutes.

DARK CHOCOLATE TOFU CREAM

- In a mixer, beat the tofu and condensed milk for a few minutes.
- Melt the chocolate in a bain-marie.
- Add the melted chocolate to the tofu mixture and beat in a food processor until homogeneous.
- Pour into the pie crust and cool in the refrigerator for 3 to 4 hours.

YOGURT AND MILK CHOCOLATE VARIATION

- Melt the chocolate in a bain-marie.
- In a mixer, beat the yogurt and gradually add the melted chocolate.
- Pour into the pie crust and let cool in the refrigerator for 3 to 4 hours.

Sunshine Two Citrus Pie

Servings: 8 to 10 | **Preparation:** 45 min | **Cooking time:** 45 min | **Refrigeration:** 1 hr
Utensil: 14 x 5" (36 x 13 cm) rectangular pan with a removable bottom

TOFU AND TWO-SESAME CRUST

- Preheat the oven to 350°F (180°C).
- Sift the baking powder with the flour.
- Mix all the crust ingredients by hand and make a ball of dough.
- Place this in the centre of the pan and spread it out evenly with your fingers, from the centre to the outside of the pan.
- Cover the dough with parchment paper. Place 2 cups (500 ml) of dried peas on top of it (this helps to keep the dough in place while baking).
- Bake the pie crust in the oven for 30 minutes.
- Remove the peas and the parchment paper. Continue to bake for 15 minutes, until the crust is golden brown.
- Take it out the oven and cool for about 30 minutes at room temperature.

ORANGE GELÉE

- Let the gelatin bloom in 1 tablespoon (15 ml) of cold water for about 5 minutes.
- In a pot, bring the orange juice to a boil.
- Dissolve the sugar into the boiling juice. While stirring, add the gelatin. Pour the hot liquid onto the egg yolks and whisk.
- Pour onto the tofu crust and let set in the refrigerator for about 30 minutes.

GRAPEFRUIT GELÉE

- Let the gelatin bloom in 1 tablespoon (15 ml) of cold water for about 5 minutes.
- In a pot, bring the grapefruit juice to a boil.
- Dissolve the sugar in the boiling juice. While stirring, add the gelatin. Pour the hot liquid onto the egg yolks and whisk.
- Let the mixture cool to room temperature for 30 minutes. Pour it over the set orange gelée. Put it back in the refrigerator for 30 minutes.

FINISHING

- Section the citrus (method on page 166).
- Garnish the pie with the supremes.

INGREDIENTS

TOFU AND TWO-SESAME CRUST

- 1 cup + 2 tbsp (280 ml) unbleached flour
- 1 pinch baking powder
- 1/2 cup (125 ml) firm tofu, crumbled
- 1/3 cup (80 ml) cane sugar
- 1 egg, beaten
- 2 tsp (10 ml) sesame oil
- 1 tbsp (15 ml) white sesame seeds
- 1 tbsp (15 ml) black sesame seeds

ORANGE GELÉE

- 1/2 package (1 tsp) or 5 ml gelatin
- 1 tbsp (15 ml) cold water
- 1 cup (250 ml) orange juice, freshly squeezed
- 1/2 cup (125 ml) cane sugar
- 4 egg yolks, beaten

GRAPEFRUIT GELÉE

- 1/2 package (1 tsp) or 5 ml gelatin
- 1 tbsp (15 ml) cold water
- 1 cup (250 ml) grapefruit juice, freshly squeezed
- 1/2 cup (125 ml) cane sugar
- 4 egg yolks, beaten

FINISHING

- 2 oranges
- 2 grapefruits

INGREDIENTS

SWEET PASTRY CRUMB CRUST

- 1 cup (250 ml) sweet pastry crumbs (recipe on page 14)
- 2 tbsp (15 ml) unsalted butter, melted

COCONUT FONDANT

- 1/4 cup (60 ml) 35% cream
- 1/2 cup (125 ml) milk chocolate, chopped
- 1/2 cup (125 ml) unsweetened coconut, grated and toasted

MASCARPONE CREAM

- 1 cup (250 ml) mascarpone cheese
- 2 tbsp (30 ml) honey
- 2 egg yolks

MANGO AND PINEAPPLE FILLING

- 1/2 fresh pineapple, cut into 1/2" (1 cm) cubes
- 1 tbsp (15 ml) unsalted butter
- 1 tbsp (15 ml) cane sugar
- 1 mango, cut into 1/2" (1 cm) cubes
- 1 tsp (5 ml) ginger, freshly grated

Creamy Coco-Mango-Pineapple Pie

Servings: 6 to 8 I **Preparation:** 45 min I **Cooking time:** 10 min I **Refrigeration** 1 hr 30 min
Utensil: 9" (23 cm) round pie plate with a removable bottom.

Each mouthful of this pie takes you on a fantastic journey of flavours and textures. It awakens your palate with joyous sensations—from the voluptuous consistency of Italian mascarpone to the tropical exoticism and firm tenderness of mango and pineapple.

SWEET PASTRY CRUMB CRUST (MAKE THE NIGHT BEFORE)

- In a bowl, mix the crumbs and the butter by hand until it creates a crust.
- Line the bottom of the pan with parchment paper. Line with the crumb mixture and press well, without nudging it up the sides.
- Bake in the oven at 350°F (180°C) for 10 minutes.

COCONUT FONDANT

- Without bringing to a boil, heat the cream and carefully pour over the chocolate in a bowl. Mix with a wooden spoon until the chocolate melts.
- Mix in the coconut and carefully pour over the chilled crust.
- Chill in the fridge for 1 hour. Turn it out and place it on a serving dish.

MASCARPONE CREAM

- In a pot, heat the cheese and honey on low heat.
- Whisk in the egg yolks vigorously for 3 minutes, then emulsify with a hand-held blender for 2 minutes.
- Let cool for 1 hour and 30 minutes in the refrigerator.
- Cover the fondant with the mascarpone cream.

MANGO AND PINEAPPLE FILLING

- In a pan on medium-high heat, sauté the pineapple cubes with the butter and sugar for 10 minutes, stirring constantly so the caramelization is even.
- Add the mangoes and ginger and continue to cook for 5 minutes.
- Let the fruit cool through and garnish the top of the pie.
- Serve with chocolate sauce or custard (recipes on page 156).

Multifruit Pie

Servings: 6 to 8 | **Preparation:** 30 min | **Cooking time:** none
Refrigeration: 2 hrs | **Utensil:** 10" (25 cm) round pie plate, Pyrex or ceramic

With no cooking time, no fat and no added sugar, this pie is very healthy and ultra-flavourful. It is a creation like no other and is easy to make. Check it out!

DRIED FRUIT AND ALMOND CRUST

- Grind the almonds in a food processor.
- Add the other ingredients and grind again.
- With your fingers, press the mixture into the bottom of the pie plate.

FRUIT FILLING

- Arrange the fruit on top of the dried fruit and almond crust.
- In a pot, mix the fruit juice with the agar agar and bring to a boil.
- Turn the heat down and simmer gently for 5 to 10 minutes, or until the flakes are completely dissolved.
- Mix well. Pour the hot mixture into the fruit.
- Chill in the refrigerator for 2 hours and serve.

INGREDIENTS

DRIED FRUIT AND ALMOND CRUST

- 1 1/2 cups (375 ml) whole almonds, toasted
- 1 1/2 cups (375 ml) dried fruits (a mix of dates, figs, and raisins)
- 1 tsp (5 ml) ground cinnamon
- 1 tbsp (15 ml) water (or more if needed)

FRUIT FILLING

- 3 to 4 cups (750 ml-1 L) fruit of your choice (strawberries, blueberries, kiwis, cherries, blackberries, white grapes or others)
- 2 cups (500 ml) cran-raspberry juice or another fruit juice
- 2 tbsp (30 ml) agar agar flakes (sold in health-food stores)

DOMINIQUE'S ADVICE

If you choose fruit that oxidizes quickly, such as apples and pears, pour lemon over them as soon as they are cut into cubes. The lemon juice will stop oxidization.

INGREDIENTS

OATMEAL AND
HAZELNUT CRUST

- 1 1/3 cups (330 ml) whole hazelnuts
- 1 cup (250 ml) oatmeal
- 1/4 tsp (1 ml) sea salt
- 2 tbsp (30 ml) canola oil
- 1/4 cup (60 ml) water
- 1/4 cup (60 ml) honey, heated (to a liquid)

CHOCOLATE AND
HAZELNUT SPREAD

- 1/2 cup (125 ml) hazelnuts, toasted
- 1 tbsp (15 ml) honey
- 3 tbsp (45 ml) cocoa powder
- 1 tsp (5 ml) pure vanilla extract
- 1/4 cup (80 ml) milk powder
- 1/4 cup (60 ml) milk or water

FILLING

- 1/4 cup (60 ml) dark chocolate, chopped
- 2 bananas, sliced

DOMINIQUE'S ADVICE

If you want to make the pie in advance, sprinkle lemon juice on the bananas so they don't brown.

Banana-Hazelnut-Chocolate Pie

Servings: 6 to 8 | **Preparation:** 40 min | **Cooking time:** 50 min | **Utensil:** Cookie sheet

This fresh pie is warm in the sense that it is a wonderfully comforting dessert in winter. It is extremely nourishing and stands out by virtue of a mix of rich ingredients and the fresh taste of succulent bananas.

OATMEAL AND HAZELNUT CRUST

- Preheat the oven to 300^{0}F (150^{0}C).
- Grind the hazelnuts in a food processor until they are the size of oatmeal.
- Mix the oatmeal, ground hazelnuts and salt in a bowl.
- In a different bowl, beat oil, water and honey with a fork. Add it to the dry mixture.
- Let rest for 10 minutes, so the oatmeal can soak up the liquid. Make a ball of dough with your hands.
- Line a cookie sheet with parchment paper and spread out the dough with your fingers to make an 8" (20 cm) diameter crust.
- Bake the crust in the centre of the oven for 40 to 50 minutes, until it is golden.
- Cool at room temperature.

CHOCOLATE AND HAZELNUT SPREAD

- Pour all the ingredients into a food processor or mixer and grind them until the mixture is homogeneous.

FILLING

- Melt the chocolate in a bain-marie and use half of it to cover the bottom of the pie.
- Cool at room temperature.

ASSEMBLY

- Place the crust on a serving dish.
- Slather the hazelnut spread on the crust.
- Garnish the crust with the banana slices. Dribble the remaining half of the melted chocolate to form a mesh-like pattern.
- Serve with chocolate sauce (recipe on page 156).

Yogurt Mousse Fruit Tarts with Hazelnut Crust

Servings: 6 | **Preparation:** 20 min | **Cooking time:** 50 min | **Utensil:** Cookie sheet

HAZELNUT CRUST

- Preheat the oven to 300°F (150°C).
- In a mixer, whisk the egg whites to soft peaks and gradually sprinkle in the sugar.
- Add the hazelnuts with a spatula.
- Line the cookie sheet with parchment paper.
- Divide the mixture into six similar piles on the parchment paper. Flatten the piles to create 3 to 4" (8 to 10 cm) disks.
- Bake in the oven for 40 to 50 minutes, until the meringues are lightly golden.
- Cool the meringues on a rack.

YOGURT MOUSSE

- In a mixer, whisk the cream to firm peaks.
- Gently add the yogurt to the cream and set aside in the refrigerator.

FILLING

- Cut the fruit to your liking.
- Spread the yogurt mousse onto the meringues right before serving so they remain crunchy.
- Garnish with the fruit.

APPLE AND CARAMEL MOUSSE VARIATION

CARAMEL MOUSSE

- In a small pot, heat 1/2 cup (125 ml) of the cream.
- In another pot, on medium, heat the sugar with 2 tablespoons (30 ml) of water until it caramelizes (see information about caramel on page 160).
- Add the butter to the hot cream. Mix well and cool.
- In a mixer, whisk the cold cream to firm peaks.
- Gently add the caramel to the whipped cream with a spatula.

INGREDIENTS

HAZELNUT CRUST

- 2 egg whites
- 2 cups (500 ml) whole hazelnuts
- 2 tbsp (30 ml) cane sugar

YOGURT MOUSSE

- 1/3 cup (80 ml) 35% cream
- 1/2 cup (125 ml) thick plain yogurt (10 %)

FILLING

- Fresh fruit of your choice (kiwis, mangoes, peaches, cherries, etc.)

APPLE AND CARAMEL MOUSSE VARIATION CARAMEL MOUSSE

- 1/2 cup (125 ml) 35% cream, cold, for the mousse
- 1/3 cup (80 ml) cane sugar
- 1/4 cup (60 ml) unsalted butter
- 1 cup (250 ml) 35% cream

INGREDIENTS

APPLE FILLING

- 2 medium Cortland, Empire, Golden or Lobo apples, cored, peeled and diced into 1/2" (1cm) pieces
- 1 tbsp (15 ml) unsalted butter
- 1 tbsp (15 ml) cane sugar

DOMINIQUE'S ADVICE

Make sure that the cream is hot before pouring it into the hot caramel. If it is cold or warm, it could splatter and cause burns. As the saying goes, better safe than sorry.

APPLE FILLING

- In a non-stick pan, caramelize the diced apples with the butter and sugar until no liquid remains.
- Cool for 30 minutes at room temperature.

ASSEMBLY

- Spread the caramel mousse on the meringues right before serving so they remain crunchy.
- Garnish the mousse with the caramelized apples.

INGREDIENTS

- 1/2 cup (125 ml) 35% cream
- 1 tbsp (15 ml) cocoa powder

- 1/2 cup (125 ml) water
- 2/3 cup (160 ml) cane sugar
- 4 egg yolks
- 2 tbsp (30 ml) dark chocolate, chopped

- 2 cups (500 ml) milk chocolate, chopped
- 1 cup (250 ml) natural peanut butter, preferably chunky
- 3 cups (750 ml) puffed rice cereal

Ice Cream Sandwich Pie

Servings: 8 | **Preparation:** 45 min | **Cooking time:** 30 min | **Refrigeration:** 1 hr
Freezing time: 24 hrs | **Utensils:** Two 8 x 11" (20 to 27 cm) rectangular pans

This recipe originates from its wonderful crust, which I concocted with chocolate, peanut butter and puffed rice. After juggling many ideas to find a match for the filling, we finally transformed it into a festive frozen sandwich pie based on Dominique's inspired suggestion.

CHOCOLATE PARFAIT • COCOA CHANTILLY

- In a mixer, whip the cream and cocoa to firm peaks and set aside in the refrigerator.

CHOCOLATE PARFAIT • DARK CHOCOLATE CREAM

- In a pot, bring the water and sugar to a boil to make syrup.
- Beat the egg yolks on high with a mixer. Add the hot syrup to the beaten egg yolks. Beat the mixture to triple the volume, until it lightens in colour and firm peaks form (about 10 to 12 minutes, or until the mixture cools).
- Melt the chocolate in a bain-marie. Gradually add to the whisked egg yolks with a spatula.

MAKING THE CHOCOLATE PARFAIT

- Gradually fold the cocoa whipped cream into the chocolate cream with a spatula. Line the pan with plastic wrap and pour in the chocolate parfait. Freeze for 24 hours.

PUFFED RICE, CHOCOLATE AND PEANUT BUTTER COOKIE

- Melt the chocolate in a bain-marie.
- Put the peanut butter in a bowl and pour the melted chocolate over top. Mix together.
- Gently incorporate the puffed rice with a spatula. Do not break up the rice.
- Line the pans with plastic wrap. Spread half of the mixture into each pan, without going up the sides. Set in the refrigerator for 1 hour. The cookies can be made one after the other in the same pan.

ASSEMBLY

- Right before serving, turn out the cookies and place them in a serving dish.
- Turn out the parfait and place it on top of the cookie. Cover it with a second cookie. Cut and serve immediately.

Pear and Maple Caramelized Pecan Pie

Servings: 6 to 8 | **Preparation:** 40 min | **Cooking time:** 50 min | **Utensil:** Cookie sheet

Everything is divine in this pie: the fusion of flavours, the maple-caramelized pecans and pears, the texture of the crust, the softness of the pears...

PECAN AND OATMEAL CRUST

- Preheat the oven to 300°F (150°C).
- Grind the pecans in a food processor until they are the size of oatmeal.
- In a bowl, mix the oatmeal with the ground pecans and salt.
- In another bowl, beat the oil, water, and maple syrup with a fork. Add this to the dry mixture.
- Let it rest for 10 minutes so the oatmeal soaks up the liquid. Make a ball of dough with your hands.
- Line a cookie sheet with parchment paper and spread out the dough with your fingers to make an 8" (20 cm) diameter crust.
- Bake the crust in the centre of the oven for 40 to 50 minutes, until it is golden.
- Cool on a rack at room temperature.

MAPLE SYRUP CARAMELIZED PEARS

- In a non-stick pan, melt the butter and maple syrup on medium-high heat.
- Add the pears and let them caramelize until there is no more liquid. The pears should be golden brown.

MAPLE SYRUP CARAMELIZED PECANS

- Preheat the oven to 325°F (160°C).
- Toast the pecans for 15 minutes.
- After the pecans are toasted, turn off the heat and leave them in the hot oven.
- In a non-stick pan on high heat, bring the maple syrup to a boil. Turn down the heat to low and simmer for 2 minutes.

INGREDIENTS

PECAN AND OATMEAL CRUST

- 1 1/3 cups (330 ml) whole pecans
- 1 cup (250 ml) oatmeal
- 1/4 tsp (1 ml) sea salt
- 2 tbsp (30 ml) canola oil
- 1/4 cup (60 ml) water
- 1/4 cup (60 ml) maple syrup

MAPLE SYRUP CARAMELIZED PEARS

- 2 tbsp (30 ml) unsalted butter
- 1/4 cup (60 ml) maple syrup
- 4 medium Bartlett pears, cored, peeled and cut into eight

INGREDIENTS

MAPLE SYRUP CARAMELIZED PECANS

- 1 cup (250 ml) pecans
- 1/4 cup (60 ml) maple syrup

FINISHING

- 1/3 cup (80 ml) milk chocolate, chopped

- Pour the hot pecans into the maple syrup and cook on low, stirring constantly until the pecans are caramelized.
- Line the cookie sheet with parchment paper. Spread out the pecans and cool.
- Once the pecans have cooled through, break the clusters if necessary.

ASSEMBLY

- Melt the chocolate in a bain-marie.
- Place the caramelized pears in a spiral on the crust and scatter the caramelized pecans on top.
- Serve with caramel sauce (recipe on page 156).

INGREDIENTS

TULIP CRUST

- 2 1/2 tbsp (40 ml) unsalted butter, soft
- 1/3 cup + 1 tbsp (95 ml) cane sugar
- 1 tsp (5 ml) pure vanilla extract
- 2 egg whites
- 1/3 cup (80 ml) unbleached flour
- 1/3 cup (80 ml) milk chocolate, chopped

FILLING

- 1 cup (250 ml) 35% cream
- 1 1/2 tbsp (25 ml) cane sugar
- Fresh fruit of your choice

Tulip-Shaped Seasonal Fruit Pie

Servings: 8 | **Preparation:** 30 min | **Cooking time:** 15 min
Utensils: cookie sheet and eight 2" (5 cm) round glasses

TULIP CRUST

- Preheat the oven to 350°F (180°C).
- In a bowl, mix the butter, sugar and vanilla with a spatula.
- Add the egg whites, followed by the flour. Mix well to obtain a smooth batter.
- Line the cookie sheet with parchment paper, and using a soup spoon, make two 5 1/2" (14 cm) rounds of batter.
- Bake the batter for 5 minutes, take out of the oven, flip the cookies, and put back into the oven for 3 minutes, or until golden brown.
- Take the cookies out of the oven and immediately place each cookie on an overturned glass to give it a tulip shape.
- Repeat the steps three times until you have eight tulips.
- Cool at room temperature.
- Once the tulips have cooled, melt the chocolate in a bain-marie.
- Brush the insides of the tulips with the melted chocolate.

FILLING

- Whisk cream and sugar to a thick cream and fill the tulips halfway.
- Garnish with your choice of fruit.

Quick Eggs in Milk Pie

Servings: 6 to 8 | **Preparation:** 15 min | **Cooking time:** 20 min | **Refrigeration:** 1 h
Utensil: 9" (23 cm) round pie plate, Pyrex or ceramic

Here is another of my favourites. Easy and quick to prepare, this pie is a real joy to eat. Delicious on demand, it is extremely refreshing when served cold. A must to discover if you haven't already. This is an ideal summer dessert!

- Preheat the oven to 400⁰F (200⁰C).
- In a pot, heat the milk until the point of boiling.
- In a bowl, whisk the eggs and sugar together.
- Add the hot milk, then the butter, to the egg mixture.
- Pour into the pan and bake for 20 minutes, or until it has set.
- Dust with 2 tablespoons (30 ml) of sugar. Place under the broiler for 1 to 2 minutes to caramelize the sugar.
- Refrigerate for 1 hour.
- Serve cold, accompanied by fresh fruit or raspberry coulis (recipe on page 156).

Gourmet Note

For a tastier pie, dust with vanilla sugar instead of cane sugar (recipe on page 170).

- 2 cups (500 ml) milk
- 1/2 cup + 2 tbsp (155 ml) cane sugar
- 5 eggs
- 4 tsp (20 ml) unsalted butter

CREATIVE PIES

Caution: you are entering culinary heaven. We warn you that is is possible that you will become addicted. Extremely possible. In this section, we wanted to take the mystery out of the art of pastry making—to make it as accessible as possible. And so, with passion and without pretension, we invite you to a veritable festival of flavours where we approach pie-making in the same spectacular way as with cakes. Dacquoise, sponge cake, praline, truffles...all it takes is hard work! The good part about pies is that there is no need to worry about creativity versus aesthetic, as with cakes. The less round pies are, the more they have a homemade feel. This section provides hours of pleasure in baking, for all levels of gourmets, from the skilled to the not-so-skilled. Creativity never tasted so good.

Orange Tenderness

Servings: 6 to 8 | **Preparation:** 50 min | **Cooking time:** 25 min | **Refrigeration:** 20 min
Utensil: 9" (23 cm) round fluted tart pan with a removable bottom

This pie is inspired by Dominique's mother's improvised last-minute dessert. Originally, it was a pound cake she made by measuring out the ingredients with a yogurt container. The cake was made with equal parts eggs, flour, sugar and plain yogurt instead of butter. Putting his talents as a pastry chef to good use, Dominique reinvented this dessert to transform it into an orange pie. It is wonderfully delicious and worthy of his childhood memories.

YOGURT AND ORANGE POUND CAKE CRUST
- Preheat the oven to 350°F (180°C).
- Beat the eggs and the sugar with a whisk until the mixture is frothy. Gradually add, in this order, the yogurt, flour, and zest. Mix with a spatula.
- Grease and flour the pan. Pour in the mixture.
- Bake in the oven (about 25 minutes) until a toothpick comes out clean from the middle of the crust. Turn out the crust onto a rack and cool.

WHITE CHOCOLATE MOUSSE
- In a pot, heat the milk on medium without bringing to a boil.
- Let the gelatin bloom in 2 tablespoons (30 ml) of cold water for about 5 minutes.
- Beat the egg yolks and sugar with a whisk until the mixture is frothy. Add the hot milk. Put everything back into the pot and cook for 2 minutes, stirring constantly with a spatula.
- Put the chopped chocolate in a bowl and pour over the hot mixture. Add the gelatin and mix with a hand-held blender to emulsify.
- Chill in the refrigerator for about 20 minutes. The gelatin should not set, but it should be cold.
- Whip the cream and carefully fold it into the white chocolate preparation. Set aside in the refrigerator.

FINISHING
- With a piping bag, make balls of white chocolate mousse and place them on the pound cake crust.
- Section the oranges (method on page 166) and place them around the balls of mousse. Decorate with candied orange peels (recipe on page 149), if you like.

INGREDIENTS

YOGURT AND ORANGE POUND CAKE CRUST
- 3 eggs
- 2/3 cup (160 ml) cane sugar
- 1/2 cup (125 ml) plain yogurt
- 2/3 cup (160 ml) unbleached flour
- Zest of 3 medium oranges

WHITE CHOCOLATE MOUSSE
- 1 cup (250 ml) milk
- 1 package gelatin (10 ml or 2 tsp)
- 4 egg yolks
- 1/2 cup + 2 tbsp (155 ml) cane sugar
- 1/4 cup (60 ml) white chocolate, chopped
- 1 cup (250 ml) 35% cream

FINISHING
- 5 oranges

INGREDIENTS

- 1 Quick Puff Pastry recipe (see page 15-16)
- 2 tbsp (30 ml) cane sugar
- 1/2 tsp (2.5 ml) ground cinnamon

SAUTÉED APPLES AND CINNAMON FILLING

- 4 medium Cortland, Empire, Golden or Lobo apples, cored, peeled and diced
- 2 tbsp (30 ml) cane sugar
- 1 tsp (5 ml) ground cinnamon

WHIPPED CREAM

- 1/2 a vanilla pod
- 3/4 cup (175 ml) 35% cream
- 2 tbsp (30 ml) cane sugar

Sautéed Apples and Cinnamon Clouds

Servings: 8 to 10 | **Preparation:** 45 min | **Cooking time:** 25 min | **Utensil:** Cookie sheet

PUFF PASTRY CRUST

- Preheat the oven to 400°F (200°C).
- Separate the puff pastry into four equal pieces.*
- Flour the work surface and roll out one of the pieces of dough to make a 14 x 5″ (36 x 13 cm) strip. To get a nicely shaped rectangle, roll out the dough lengthwise with the rolling pin first, then cut out the rectangle with a knife to the precise dimensions.
- Line the cookie sheet with parchment paper. Place the rolled-out pastry on it.
- Mix the sugar with the cinnamon, brush the dough with water, and dust it with the mixture. Let it rest for 30 minutes.
- Bake in the oven for 25 minutes, until the pastry is golden. The puff pastry will puff up with baking. This is normal and exactly what you want, as it indicates that the pastry is aerated, light and flaky.
- Cool on a rack at room temperature.

SAUTÉED APPLES AND CINNAMON FILLING

- Sauté the diced apples with the cinnamon sugar until all the liquid has evaporated.
- Cool at room temperature.

WHIPPED CREAM

- Cut the vanilla pod in half, scrape out the seeds with a knife and put them into the cream.
- Whip the mixture to firm peaks.

ASSEMBLY

- Spread the whipped cream onto the puff pastry crust and divide up the diced apples on top.

OPTIONAL FINISHING

- Garnish with apple crisps (recipe on page 149).

* As this recipe only requires a quarter of the quick puff pastry recipe keep the other pieces to make other pies, palmier sticks or sesame crackers (recipes on page 146). Wrapped in plastic wrap, the dough will easily last a month in the freezer.

Apple Caramel Delight

Servings: 8 to 10 | **Preparation:** 40 min | **Cooking time:** 35 min | **Refrigeration:** 30 min
Utensil: 9" (23 cm) round tart pan with a removable bottom

APPLE SPONGE CAKE CRUST

- Preheat the oven to 350°F (180°C).
- Mix the apples and cinnamon.
- With a hand-held beater, beat the egg yolks and sugar until frothy. Continue beating until the mixture has doubled in size.
- Sift the flour and corn starch together. Carefully fold it into the frothy egg yolk mixture with a spatula.
- Beat the egg whites with a hand-held beater.
- Fold the beaten egg whites into the egg yolk mixture. Add the apples.
- Pour the mixture into the pan and bake for 35 minutes, or until the cake is golden.
- Turn it out onto a rack. Cool.

APPLE MOUSSE

- In a pan on medium-high heat, cook the apples, butter and sugar until the mixture becomes a chunky jam.
- Cool in the refrigerator for 30 minutes.
- Whip the cream.
- Fold the cooled jam into the whipped cream. Set aside in the refrigerator.

SOFT NUT CARAMEL

- In a small pot, on medium, heat the cream.
- In another pot, heat the corn syrup on medium-high heat.
- In small increments, add the sugar to the hot syrup while stirring with a spatula.
- While stirring carefully, heat for 6 minutes, until a caramel forms (see information about caramel on page 160).
- Take the caramel off the heat and pour it into the hot cream while whisking.
- Continue to cook the mixture for 1 to 2 minutes on medium heat until it is thick enough to be malleable.
- Take it off the heat, add the butter and nuts. Mix.
- Let cool in the pan for 10 to 15 minutes. Place the soft caramel on the apple sponge crust.

INGREDIENTS

APPLE SPONGE CAKE CRUST

- 1 cup (250 ml) Cortland, Empire, Golden or Lobo apples, cored, peeled and cut into 1/4" (5 mm) cubes
- 1 tsp (5 ml) ground cinnamon
- 3 egg yolks
- 1/3 cup (80 ml) cane sugar
- 1/4 cup (60 ml) unbleached flour
- 1/3 cup (80 ml) corn starch
- 3 egg whites

APPLE MOUSSE

- 3 medium Cortland, Empire, Golden or Lobo apples, cored, peeled and cut into 1/4" (5 mm) cubes
- 2 tbsp (30 ml) unsalted butter
- 3 tbsp (45 ml) cane sugar
- 3/4 cup (175 ml) 35% cream

SOFT NUT CARAMEL

- 1/2 cup (125 ml) 35% cream
- 3 tbsp (45 ml) corn syrup
- 1/2 cup (125 ml) cane sugar
- 1 tbsp (15 ml) unsalted butter
- 2/3 cup (160 ml) walnuts, toasted and roughly chopped

ASSEMBLY

- With two spoons, make quenelles with the apple mousse. Place them on the caramel and serve with custard or caramel sauce (recipes on page 156).

OPTIONAL FINISHING

- Garnish with apple crisps (recipe on page 149).

DOMINIQUE'S ADVICE

Make sure the cream is hot before before pouring it into the hot caramel. If it is cold or warm, it could splatter and cause burns. As Better safe than sorry!

- 1/4 cup (60 ml) pecans, toasted
- 3/4 cup (175 ml) milk chocolate, chopped
- 2 tbsp (30 ml) unsweetened coconut, grated

COCONUT CREAM

- 3/4 cup (175 ml) coconut milk
- 1/3 cup (80 ml) unsweetened coconut, grated
- 1 egg yolk
- 2 tsp (10 ml) corn starch
- 2 tbsp (30 ml) cane sugar
- 1/4 cup (60 ml) unsalted butter

COCONUT CRISP

- 3 tbsp (45 ml) unsweetened coconut, grated
- 3 tbsp (45 ml) cane sugar
- 1 tbsp (15 ml) water

Intense Coconut Extravaganza

Servings: 6 to 8 | **Preparation:** 45 min | **Cooking time:** 15 min | **Refrigeration:** 24 hrs
Utensil: 6" (15 cm) round springform pan

CHOCOLATE, PECAN AND COCONUT CRUST

- Using a food processor, grind all the ingredients to a firm dough together with a plasticine-like texture.
- Place the dough in a pan lined with plastic wrap and spread it out with your fingers, with a 1" (2.5 cm) border.
- Cool at room temperature.

COCONUT CREAM

- In a pot, heat the coconut milk and grated coconut without bringing it to a boil.
- In a bowl, whisk the egg yolks, corn starch and sugar.
- Add the hot coconut mixture to the bowl.
- Put everything back into the pot and cook on medium heat for 2 minutes.
- Add the butter and emulsify using a hand-held blender.
- Chill in the refrigerator for 30 minutes. Pour onto the pie crust.
- Set in the refrigerator, ideally for 24 hours.

COCONUT CRISP

- Preheat the oven to 350°F (180°C) and toast the coconut for about 10 minutes.
- In a non-stick pan, cook the sugar and water on medium heat until golden, then add the toasted coconut. Mix with a wooden spoon for 3 to 4 minutes.
- Spread out the mixture on a cookie sheet or a piece of parchment paper. Cool at room temperature.
- Break up the crisp with your fingers and spread it over the top of the pie.

OPTIONAL FINISHING

- Garnish with curls of toasted coconut.

NOTE

This pie should be made the night before to give it sufficient time to set.

Indecent Praline and Chocolate Duo on a Brownie

Servings: 8 | **Preparation:** 1 hr | **Cooking time:** 35 min | **Refrigeration:** 30 hrs
Utensils: 9 x 9" (23 x 23 cm) square fluted pan with removable bottom

ALMOND AND HAZELNUT PRALINE*

- In a pot on low heat, cook all the ingredients until the almonds and hazelnuts caramelize. Stir from time to time with a wooden spoon.
- Pour the mixture onto a greased cookie sheet and cool at room temperature.
- Break the cooled mixture into pieces and grind in a food processor to obtain a creamy batter. This might take about 10 minutes on "Pulse."
- For optimal results, clean the sides of the processor frequently with a spatula.

PRALINE WHIPPED CREAM

- In a bowl, whip the cream with electric beaters until firm peaks form.
- In another bowl, gently fold the praline into a third of the whipped cream until it is totally deflated.
- As soon as the fragments of praline are well distributed, fold in the rest of the whipped cream with a spatula.
- Chill in the refrigerator for 30 minutes.

BROWNIE CRUST

- Preheat the oven to 350°F (180°C).
- In a bowl, mix the cocoa and baking soda with a spatula. Add half of the butter and mix well.
- Gradually add the boiling water, sugar, egg, and the rest of the butter. Mix well. Add the flour, salt, chocolate chips and vanilla. Mix.
- Grease the pan and dust uniformly with 1 tablespoon (15 ml) of cocoa powder. Distribute it evenly over the entire surface of the pan. Turn the pan upside down and tap it to remove the extra cocoa.
- Pour the chocolate mixture into the pan and bake for 35 minutes. Cool at room temperature.

* This praline recipe produces more than is required for the pie. It is hard to get a smaller quantity due to the normal capacity of food processors. Use the rest of the praline as is or mix it with melted chocolate to spread on toast or to garnish ice cream.

INGREDIENTS

ALMOND AND HAZELNUT PRALINE

- 1/3 cup (80 ml) whole almonds, toasted
- 1/3 cup (80 ml) whole hazelnuts, toasted
- 1/2 cup (125 ml) cane sugar
- 3 tbsp (45 ml) water

PRALINE WHIPPED CREAM

- 1 1/2 cups (375 ml) 35% cream
- 1/2 cup (125 ml) almond and hazelnut praline

BROWNIE CRUST

- 1/3 cup + 2 tbsp (110 ml) cocoa powder
- 1 pinch baking soda
- 1/4 cup (60 ml) unsalted butter, melted
- 1/3 cup (80 ml) boiling water
- 1 1/3 cups (330 ml) cane sugar
- 1 egg, beaten
- 1 cup (250 ml) unbleached flour
- 1 pinch sea salt
- 1/2 cup (125 ml) chocolate chips of your choice
- 1/2 tsp (2.5 ml) pure vanilla extract

TO PREPARE THE PAN

- 1 tbsp (15 ml) unsalted butter
- 1 tbsp (15 ml) cocoa powder

INGREDIENTS

GANACHE

- 1/4 cup (60 ml) milk
- 2/3 cup (160 ml) 35% cream
- 1 1/3 cup (330 ml) dark chocolate, chopped
- 1/4 cup (60 ml) unsalted butter, soft

FINISHING

- 1/2 cup (125 ml) hazelnuts, crushed and toasted

JOSÉE'S RECOMMENDATION

Cacao Barry's 56% cocoa bittersweet chocolate with its light, sweet taste, and Michel Cluizel's 64% cocoa, with its fresh notes of banana, are two excellent choices if you want to make this pie very chocolate. The first is a sweet combination while the second has more contrasting flavours.

GANACHE

- In a pot, heat the milk and cream without bringing it to a boil.
- In a bowl, carefully pour the hot mixture onto the chocolate and stir with a wooden spoon until the chocolate is completely melted.
- Add the butter and emulsify with a hand-held blender for 30 seconds to get homogeneous ganache.
- Let the ganache cool in the refrigerator for 45 minutes, until it is malleable.

FINISHING

- Use a piping bag to make praline whip cream and ganache balls. Alternate them as garnish on the brownie in a checkerboard pattern.
- Garnish with toasted crushed hazelnuts.

- 3 egg yolks
- 1/3 cup (80 ml) cane sugar
- 3 egg whites
- 1/4 cup (60 ml) unbleached flour
- 2 tbsp (30 ml) corn starch
- 2 tbsp (30 ml) cocoa powder

TO PREPARE THE PAN

- 1 tbsp (15 ml) unsalted butter
- 1 tbsp (15 ml) cocoa powder

LEMON WHIPPED CREAM

- 1/3 cup (80 ml) 35% cream
- 2 tbsp (30 ml) mascarpone cheese
- 1 tbsp (15 ml) cane sugar
- Zest of 3 whole lemons

FILLING

- 1 cup (250 ml) fresh raspberries

OPTIONAL FINISHING

- Raspberry coulis
- Candied lemon peels

DOMINIQUE'S ADVICE

Use a Microplane Zester to grate the zest. This kitchen utensil finds only the aromatic part of the citrus.

Fascinating Chocolate-Lemon-Raspberries Fusion

Servings: 6 to 8 | **Preparation:** 1 hr | **Cooking time:** 25 min
Utensil: 8" (20 cm) round fluted tart pan with a removable bottom

CHOCOLATE SPONGE CAKE CRUST

- Preheat the oven to 350°F (180°C).
- With a mixer, beat the egg yolks and sugar until the mixture is frothy and doubles in volume.
- In another bowl, whip the egg whites to soft peaks.
- Mix together the flour, corn starch and cocoa powder.
- Add the dry ingredients to the egg yolk mixture. Beat well to make a homogeneous mixture.
- Fold the egg yolk mixture into the egg whites with a spatula.
- Grease the pan, dust with 1 tablespoon (15 ml) of cocoa powder and distribute it over the entire surface of the pan.
- Turn the pan upside down and tap it to remove the extra cocoa.
- Pour the mixture into the pan and bake for 25 minutes. The crust is perfectly baked when a toothpick inserted in the cake comes out clean.
- Turn it out and cool on a rack.

LEMON WHIPPED CREAM

- With a hand-held beater, whip all the ingredients to get firm whipped cream.

FILLING

- Spread the lemon whipped cream on the sponge cake crust.
- Garnish with fresh raspberries and serve with raspberry coulis (recipe on page 156). To please the eyes as much as the palate, as would a top chef, follow the proposed optional finishing.

OPTIONAL FINISHING

- Once the coulis is made, strain it to remove the seeds. Chill in the refrigerator until it has thickened.
- With the tip of a knife, place small drops of coulis in the cavity of each raspberry.
- Garnish with candied lemon peels (recipe on page 149).

Mango Strawberry Delight

Servings: 8 to 10 | **Preparation:** 1 hr | **Cooking time:** 35 min | **Refrigeration:** 6 hrs | **Freezing:** 2 hrs
Utensils: 8" (20 cm) round spring form pan with a removable bottom and a 7" (18 cm) bowl

ALMOND DACQUOISE CRUST

- Preheat the oven to 350°F (180°C).
- In a bowl, mix the almond powder and 3 tablespoons (45 ml) of icing sugar.
- With beaters, whip the egg whites to firm peaks. Gradually add the rest of the icing sugar (3 tablespoons), followed by the almond powder mixture.
- Pour into the pan and bake for 35 minutes, or until a toothpick inserted into the cake comes out clean.
- Turn out and cool on a rack.

MANGO MOUSSE

- In a food processor, purée the mango and filter it through a strainer to get a smooth texture.
- Let the gelatin bloom for 5 minutes in 1 tablespoon (15 ml) of cold water.
- In a pot, heat the purée without bringing it to a boil and add the gelatin. Stir well.
- Let cool in the refrigerator for 1 hour, until the mixture is cold, but not set.
- With a hand-held beater, whip the cream, mascarpone and sugar until the mixture is firm. With a spatula, fold in the mango purée to the whipped mixture.
- Line the bowl with plastic wrap and pour in the mousse.
- Put into the freezer for 2 hours, until the mousse is totally set and makes a dome once turned out.

STRAWBERRY MINT GELÉE

- In a pot, heat the strawberries and sugar on low for 5 minutes. Remove from heat and cover the pot.
- Let the gelatin bloom for 5 minutes in 2 tablespoons (30 ml) of cold water.
- Strain the strawberries and reserve the juice.
- Add the gelatin and the mint leaves to the juice. Mix well.
- Cover with plastic wrap and let the mint infuse for about 30 minutes.

INGREDIENTS

ALMOND DACQUOISE CRUST

- 1 cup + 1 tbsp (265 ml) almond powder
- 1/3 cup (80 ml) icing sugar
- 4 egg whites

MANGO MOUSSE

- 1 1/4 cups (310 ml) ripe mangoes (1 to 2 mangoes depending on the size), peeled and cut into pieces
- 1/2 package (1 tsp) or 5 ml gelatin
- 1/3 cup (80 ml) 35% cream
- 2 tbsp (30 ml) mascarpone cheese
- 1 tbsp (15 ml) cane sugar

STRAWBERRY MINT GELÉE

- 3 cups (750 ml) strawberries, quartered
- 1/3 cup + 1 tbsp (95 ml) cane sugar
- 1 package gelatin (2 tsp or 10 ml)
- 25 fresh mint leaves, chopped

Strain the juice.

- Mix the reserved juice with the cooked strawberries.
- Cool in the refrigerator for 1 hour to give the strawberries shine.
- Remove the strawberries from the gelée. Set aside in the refrigerator.
- Put the gelée back into the refrigerator in a shallow flat-bottomed 9" (23 cm) container until it has set (about 4 hours).

ASSEMBLY

- Turn out the mango mousse and place it in the centre of the dacquoise crust.
- Place the strawberries, in a spiral, on the mousse.
- Break up the strawberry gelée into shards with a knife.
- Decorate the top of the pie with the shards of gelée and mint leaves.
- Put it back into the refrigerator for 2 to 3 hours before serving.

INGREDIENTS

CHOCOLATE
CRUMBLE CRUST

- 1/4 cup (60 ml) cane sugar
- 1/3 cup (80 ml) unsalted butter, soft
- 1/2 cup + 2 tbsp (155 ml) unbleached flour
- 1 pinch sea salt
- 2 tbsp (30 ml) cocoa powder

ORANGE PASTRY CREAM

- 1/2 cup (125 ml) orange juice, freshly squeezed
- 1 egg
- 2 tbsp (30 ml) cane sugar
- 1 tbsp (15 ml) corn starch
- 1/4 cup (60 ml) 35% cream

FINISHING

- 3 oranges

Orange Supremes on Chocolate Crumble

Servings: 6 to 8 | **Preparation:** 45 min | **Cooking time:** 10 min | **Refrigeration:** 15 min
Utensils: 8" (20 cm) round tart pan with a removable bottom and a cookie sheet

CHOCOLATE CRUMBLE CRUST

- Preheat the oven to 325°F (160°C).
- In a bowl, mix all the ingredients by hand to obtain homogeneous dough.
- Line the cookie sheet with parchment paper.
- Take a third of the dough and scatter it on parchment paper to make the crumble. Set aside.
- Line the bottom, not the sides, of the tart pan with the rest of the dough.
- Bake the crumble and the pie crust for 10 minutes. (If the crumble is not baked enough, it will crumble easily).

ORANGE PASTRY CREAM

- In a pot, bring the orange juice to a boil.
- In a bowl, whisk the egg, sugar and corn starch.
- Pour the hot juice onto the mixture and whisk.
- Put the mixture back into the pot and continue to cook for 1 to 2 minutes, until it is thick.
- Remove from heat and cool in the refrigerator for 15 minutes.
- With beaters, whip the cream to stiff peaks.
- Add the chilled orange preparation to the whipped cream.

FINISHING

- Section the oranges (method on page 166).
- Pour the orange pastry cream onto the crust and cover it with the crumble.
- Decorate with the orange supremes.

Celestial Spell of Grapefruit and White Chocolate

Servings: 8 to 10 | **Preparation:** 50 min | **Cooking time:** None
Refrigeration: 6 hrs | **Utensils:** 9 x 9" (23 x 23 cm) square cake pan

CRUNCHY PUFFED RICE AND WHITE CHOCOLATE CRUST

- Melt the white chocolate in a bain-marie and mix with the puffed rice.
- Line a pan with parchment paper and pour in the mixture. Chill in the refrigerator for 30 minutes.

GRAPEFRUIT CREAM

- Let the gelatin bloom in 1 tablespoon (15 ml) of cold water for 5 minutes.
- In a pot, heat the grapefruit juice.
- In a bowl, gently mix the egg yolks and the sugar with a wooden spoon.
- While gently stirring, pour the hot grapefruit juice onto the preparation.
- Put the mixture back into the pot and cook for 2 minutes on medium heat, while stirring gently with a spatula. Take the pot off the heat, add the gelatin and carefully mix until it has completely dissolved.
- Chill for 20 minutes in the refrigerator, until the cream is cold, but not set.
- Pour it onto the crust in the pan and refrigerate for 1 hour.

WHITE CHOCOLATE MOUSSE

- In a pot, heat the cream without bringing it to a boil.
- In a bowl, pour the hot cream over the chocolate and mix to melt it. Chill in the refrigerator for 6 hours.
- With a hand-held blender, whip the cooled chocolate cream to stiff peaks.

ASSEMBLY

- Turn out the crust covered with the grapefruit cream and place it on a serving dish.
- Using a piping bag, decorate the grapefruit cream with balls of white chocolate mousse.
- Section the grapefruit (method on page 166) and use it to decorate the pie.

INGREDIENTS

CRUNCHY PUFFED RICE AND WHITE CHOCOLATE CRUST

- 1/2 cup (125 ml) white chocolate, chopped
- 2 cups (500 ml) puffed rice cereal

GRAPEFRUIT CREAM

- 1/2 package gelatin (1 tsp or 5 ml)
- 1 cup (250 ml) ruby red grapefruit juice, freshly squeezed (about 2 grapefruits)
- 4 egg yolks
- 1/2 cup (125 ml) cane sugar

WHITE CHOCOLATE MOUSSE

- 1 cup (250 ml) 35% cream
- 1/3 cup (80 ml) white chocolate, chopped

FINISHING

- 1 ruby red grapefruit

- 1 cup (250 ml) raisins
- 1 cup (250 ml) boiling water
- 1/2 cup (125 ml) milk chocolate, chopped
- 1/2 cup (125 ml) almond butter
- 1 cup (250 ml) slivered almonds, toasted

DARK CHOCOLATE AND
COFFEE CREAM

- 1 cup (250 ml) 35% cream
- 1/3 cup (80 ml) coffee, finely ground
- 3/4 cup (175 ml) dark chocolate, chopped

FINISHING

- 1 cup (250 ml) 35% cream
- 1 tsp (5 ml) cocoa powder

DOMINIQUE'S ADVICE

If the dark chocolate and coffee cream mix is too sticky to spread, use the back of a wet spoon or lightly coat your fingers with neutral oil to do it.

JOSÉE'S RECOMMENDATION

For a silky blend between the coffee and chocolate, 56% cocoa dark chocolate from Valrhona is an exquisite choice.

Cappuccino Dolce Vita

Servings: 6 to 8 | **Preparation:** 45 min | **Cooking time:** 25 min | **Refrigeration:** 1 hr
Utensil: 8" (20 cm) round tart pan with removable bottom

If you love coffee, the intense coffee flavour of this pie will surely pleasure your palate. And, if you also like chocolate, you will be doubly satisfied! Life really is sweet sometimes...

MILK CHOCOLATE, RAISIN AND ALMOND CRUST

- Soak the raisins for 30 minutes in boiling water. Drain them well.
- Melt the chocolate in a bain-marie.
- In a bowl, mix the melted chocolate and the almond butter.
- Add the toasted slivered almonds and drained raisins to the bowl. Mix to obtain a ball of dough.
- Line the pan with plastic wrap and spread out the dough evenly with your fingers to the sides or even up them.
- Refrigerate for 30 minutes and then turn it out.

DARK CHOCOLATE AND COFFEE CREAM

- In a pot, on medium, bring the cream and ground coffee to a boil.
- Remove from heat and let it infuse for 10 minutes. Bring to a boil for the second time.
- Pour the hot cream through a fine mesh strainer onto the chocolate.
- Carefully stir with a wooden spoon to completely melt the chocolate. Emulsify the mixture with a hand-held blender.
- Let cool in the refrigerator for 1 hour.
- Once the cream is chilled, spread it over the bottom of the pie.

FINISHING

- With a hand-held beater, whip the cream and cover the top of the pie using a piping bag.
- Dust the whipped cream with cocoa powder.
- For a final taste of chocolate, serve this pie with chocolate sauce (recipe on page 156).

Sweet Dreams of Bananas and Chocolate

Servings: 6 to 8 | **Preparation:** 1 hr | **Cooking time:** 25 min **Resting time for dough:** 2 hrs
Refrigeration: 12 hrs | **Utensil:** Cookie sheet

PUFF PASTRY CRUST

- Separate the puff pastry into two equal pieces.*
- Flour the work surface and roll out one of the pieces of dough to make a 9" (23 cm) diameter round pie crust.
- Place the rolled-out pastry onto the cookie sheet and let rest in the refrigerator for 2 hours.
- Preheat the oven to 400°F (200°C).
- Brush the dough with water and dust with sugar.
- Bake for 25 minutes or until the dough is cooked through.
- If it puffs up during baking, pierce the bubbles with a sharp knife.
- Cool on a rack.

NOTE

Prepare the chocolate whipped cream the night before to simplify putting the pie together.

CHOCOLATE WHIPPED CREAM

- In a pot, heat the cream and sugar without bringing it to a boil.
- In a bowl, pour the hot mixture over the chocolate. Mix well to melt all the chocolate. Refrigerate for 12 hours before whipping.
- In a mixer, whip the cooled chocolate cream to stiff peaks.
- Put back into the refrigerator.

GANACHE

- In a pot, heat the milk and cream without bringing it to a boil.
- Pour the mixture over the chocolate to melt it. Add the butter and emulsify for 30 seconds with a hand-held blender to obtain a homogeneous ganache.
- Let cool for 2 hours at room temperature or until the consistency is malleable.

* As this dessert only requires half of the quick puff pastry recipe, keep the other piece of pastry to make another pie, palmier sticks or sesame crackers (recipes on page 146). Wrapped in plastic wrap, the dough will easily last a month in the freezer.

INGREDIENTS

PUFF PASTRY CRUST
- 1 Quick Puff Pastry recipe (see page 15-16)
- 1 tbsp (15 ml) cane sugar

CHOCOLATE WHIPPED CREAM
- 1 cup (250 ml) 35% cream
- 2 tbsp (30 ml) cane sugar
- 1/3 cup (80 ml) dark chocolate, chopped

GANACHE
- 2 tbsp (30 ml) milk
- 1/3 cup (80 ml) 35% cream
- 2/3 cup (160 ml) dark chocolate, chopped
- 1/4 cup (60 ml) unsalted butter, soft

INGREDIENTS

CARAMELIZED BANANA FILLING

- 4 bananas, cut in half lengthwise and cut in two widthwise
- 2 tbsp (30 ml) unsalted butter
- 2 tbsp (30 ml) cane sugar

CARAMELIZED BANANA FILLING

- Without mixing, in a non-stick pan on medium heat, melt the butter and sugar.
- Add the bananas and mix everything by moving the pan around in a circular motion. Alternate on and off the heat to ensure the melted butter and the sugar mix with the bananas. Continue swirling the ingredients until caramelization is complete. Dot no use utensils for this; it could cause the caramel to seize. Cool.

ASSEMBLY

- On the puff pastry crust, spread the ganache and place the bananas on top. Garnish with the chocolate whipped cream with a piping bag or a spoon. For a total delight, serve with custard (recipe on page 156).

INGREDIENTS

CRANBERRIES IN SYRUP

- 1/4 cup (60 ml) water
- 1/2 cup (125 ml) cane sugar
- 1/2 cup (125 ml) cranberries, fresh or frozen

ALMONDS WRAPPED IN GANACHE CRUST

- 1/4 cup (60 ml) 35% cream
- 2/3 cup (160 ml) dark chocolate, chopped
- 3/4 cup (175 ml) sliced almonds, toasted

MASCARPONE WHIPPED CREAM

- 1/3 cup (80 ml) 35% cream
- 1/3 cup (80 ml) mascarpone cheese
- 1 tbsp (15 ml) cane sugar

JOSÉE'S RECOMMENDATION

With acidic and fruit notes, 64% cocoa Manjari chocolate from Valrhona blends wonderfully with cranberries.

Small Sweets Set with Candied Cranberries

Servings: 4 I **Preparation:** 45 min I **Cooking time:** None I **Maceration:** 24 hrs (for the cranberries)
Refrigeration: 1 hr I **Utensils:** 4 individual 4 1/2 x 2 1/2" (12 x 6 cm) rectangular tart pans with removable bottom

CRANBERRIES IN SYRUP

- In a pot, boil the water and sugar.
- Pour the hot syrup into an airtight container and add the cranberries (they should be totally submerged).
- Place the lid on the container and let macerate for 24 hours in the refrigerator.

NOTE

Make the cranberries the night before so they'll be well candied.

ALMONDS WRAPPED IN GANACHE CRUST

- In a pot, heat the cream without bringing it to a boil.
- In a bowl, carefully pour the hot cream onto the chocolate and mix with a wooden spoon to completely melt it.
- Mix it all for 30 seconds with a hand-held blender to get homogeneous ganache.
- Divide half of the almonds into the four pans (if you are using pans without a removable bottom, line with plastic wrap).
- In equal parts, pour the ganache over the almonds while it is still hot.
- Divide up the rest of the toasted almonds onto the ganache in each pan.
- Refrigerate for about 1 hour, or until the crusts harden. Turn them out of the pans.

MASCARPONE WHIPPED CREAM

- In a blender, whip all the ingredients together to form a whipped cream.

ASSEMBLY

- Make whipped cream rosettes on the almond ganache crust with a piping bag.
- Garnish the top of the whipped cream with the drained candied cranberries.

Infinite Delirium of Chocolate, Sesame and Truffles

Servings: 6 to 8 | **Preparation:** 1 hr | **Cooking time:** None | **Refrigeration:** 6 hrs
Utensil: 14 x 5" (36 x 13 cm) rectangular fluted pan with a removable bottom

This pie is a real gourmet treat for a chocolate addict like me. The chocolate is abundant, almost to excess. To create it, Dominque and I gave free rein to our most chocolate imaginations as we played with textures and combinations of flavours. The crust, made of sesame, sunflower seeds, chocolate and hazelnut truffles, testifies to its succulence. Fabulously soft and crunchy, this pie excites the palate. Do I have to mention again that it is one of my favourites?

CHOCOLATE SESAME AND SUNFLOWER SEED CRUST

- Melt the chocolate and butter in a bain-marie. Add the sunflower seeds and sesame seeds and remove from heat.
- Line the pan with plastic wrap and spread the chocolate mixture right up the sides. Cool for 15 minutes at room temperature until the crust is set.

HAZELNUT TRUFFLES

- In a pot, heat the cream without bringing it to a boil. Remove from heat and pour over the chocolate in a bowl. Mix to melt the chocolate completely.
- Mix with a hand-held blender for 30 seconds to get homogeneous ganache. Chill in the refrigerator for 1 hour.
- Coat the toasted hazelnuts with the cold ganache and roll them in your hands to form 3/4" (15 mm) balls. Set aside in the refrigerator so the truffles can harden.

MILK CHOCOLATE MOUSSE

- In a pot, heat the cream without bringing it to a boil.
- In a bowl, carefully pour the hot cream onto the chocolate and mix with a wooden spoon to completely melt it. Chill in the refrigerator for 6 hours.
- With a mixer, whip the chilled chocolate cream to soft peaks. Set aside in the refrigerator.

HONEY AND SESAME CRISP

- In a pot, heat the sugar and honey for 3 minutes, until the mixture turns caramel in colour. Add butter and stir until the mixture is even.

CHOCOLATE SESAME AND SUNFLOWER SEED CRUST
- 1 cup (250 ml) milk chocolate, chopped
- 2 tbsp (30 ml) unsalted butter, melted
- 1 cup (250 ml) sunflower seeds, toasted
- 1/2 cup (125 ml) sesame seeds, toasted

HAZELNUT TRUFFLES
- 1/3 cup (80 ml) 35% cream
- 3/4 cup (175 ml) milk chocolate, chopped
- 45 whole hazelnuts, toasted

MILK CHOCOLATE MOUSSE
- 1 cup (250 ml) 35% cream
- 1/3 cup (80 ml) milk chocolate, chopped

INGREDIENTS

HONEY AND SESAME CRISP

- 2 1/2 tbsp (40 ml) cane sugar
- 1 tbsp (15 ml) honey
- 1/4 cup (60 ml) unsalted butter
- 2/3 cup (160 ml) sesame seeds, toasted

- Add the sesame seeds to the mix and cook for about 2 minutes on medium heat.
- Pour the mixture onto a piece of parchment paper, cover with another piece of paper and flatten with a rolling pin to get a thin sheet of sesame.
- Remove the top piece of parchment paper and let the mixture dry on the counter until it hardens (about 10 minutes). Break the crisp into pieces by hand.

ASSEMBLY

- Pour the chocolate mousse onto the sesame and sunflower crust. Place the hazelnut truffles around the outside of the pie.
- Right before serving, decorate by placing pieces of honey and sesame crisps on top of the pie in spikes. It is important to do this right before serving so the crisps remain crunchy. The humidity of the refrigerator will soften them.
- Serve with dark chocolate sauce (recipe on page 156).

INGREDIENTS

SWEET PASTRY CRUST

- 1 Sweet Pastry recipe (see page 13)*

FILLING

- 4 cups (1 Litre) milk
- 1 vanilla pod, cut in half lengthwise
- 3/4 cup (175 ml) Arborio rice
- 1/3 cup (80 ml) honey
- 4 cups (1 L) fresh cherries, pitted and cut in two
- 1 cup (250 ml) cane sugar
- 1 package gelatin (2 tsp or 10 ml)

* As this dessert only requires half of the sweet pastry recipe, keep the other half to make another pie. Wrapped in plastic wrap, the dough will easily last a month in the freezer.

Milk Risotto and Cherry Memories

Servings: 6 to 8 | **Preparation:** 1 hr | **Cooking time:** 45 min | **Refrigeration:** 2 hrs
Utensil: 9" (23 cm) round springform pan

This uncommon pie is a tribute to two flavours that left an impression on Dominique as a child: rice pudding, which has been renewed by risotto techniques, and cherries. As a child, Dominque liked to climb cherry trees and would stuff himself sick with cherries. That was how much he loved this fruit. This creation is the pinnacle of his fondness for these two special flavours. It's also exquisite evidence of his terrific flair for pastry.

Sweet Pastry Crust

- Preheat the oven to 350°F (180°C).
- Flour the work surface, roll out the dough with a rolling pin and line the pie plate. Or, place the ball of dough in the centre of the pie plate and spread it out evenly with your fingers from the centre to the edges (only on the bottom of the pan). Bake the crust in the oven for 45 minutes. Take out of the oven and cool for about 30 minutes.

FILLING

- In a pot, boil the milk and vanilla.
- Remove the vanilla pod, scrape the seeds out with the tip of a knife and put them back into the milk.
- In another pot on low heat, combine the rice with 1 cup (250 ml) of the
- hot milk. Stir with a wooden spoon until the rice has completely
- absorbed the milk. Add the rest of the milk 1 cup (250 ml) at a time, making sure that the rice absorbs the milk each time.
- When all the milk has been absorbed add the honey. Mix for a few minutes and remove from heat. Cool.
- In a pot, cook the cherries with the sugar on medium heat for 5 to 7 minutes. The fruit should keep its form and not turn into jam.
- During this time, let the gelatin bloom in 2 tablespoons (30 ml) of cold water for about 5 minutes. Drain the cherries, leaving the juice in the pot. Dissolve the gelatin in the hot juice and put the cherries back in. Cool.

ASSEMBLY

- Spread out the risotto evenly onto the completely cooled crust and let cool at room temperature for 45 minutes or more, until the risotto sets. Cover this with the cherries and refrigerate for 2 hours. Turn out the pie and serve with custard (recipe on page 156).

Chocolate Praline Royal Delight

Servings: 8 | **Preparation:** 1 hr | **Cooking time:** 1 hr | **Refrigeration:** 6 hrs
Utensils: 9 x 9" (23 x 23 cm) square fluted tart pan with removable bottom and a cookie sheet

SWEET PASTRY CRUST

- Preheat the oven to 350°F (180°C).
- Flour the work surface, roll out the dough with a rolling pin and line the pie plate. Or, place the ball of dough in the centre of the pie plate and spread it out evenly with your fingers from the centre to the edges.
- Cover the dough with parchment paper. Place 2 cups (500 ml) of dried peas on top of it (this helps to keep the dough in place while baking).
- Bake the pie crust in the oven for 30 minutes.
- Remove the peas and the parchment paper from the crust and continue baking for 15 minutes, until the crust is baked in the centre and it is golden brown.
- Take out of the oven and cool at room temperature for 30 minutes.

ALMOND AND NUTMEG PRALINE

- Cook all the ingredients together on low heat in a pot, stirring with a wooden spoon every once in awhile, until the almonds and hazelnuts are caramelized.
- Pour the mixture onto a greased cookie sheet and cool at room temperature.
- Break the cooled mixture into pieces and grind it in a food processor to obtain a creamy batter. It might take about 10 minutes of pulsing because the nuts need to render their natural oils for the dough to form. For optimal results, clean the sides of the processor frequently with a spatula.

DARK CHOCOLATE MOUSSE

- In a pot, heat the cream and sugar without bringing it to a boil.
- Pour the hot cream over the chocolate to completely melt it.
- Mix with a hand-held blender to obtain a uniform consistency. Chill in the refrigerator for about 6 hours.
- With a mixer, whip the chocolate cream to soft peaks. Chill in the refrigerator for 2 hours.

INGREDIENTS

SWEET PASTRY CRUST

- 1 Sweet Pastry recipe (see page 13)

ALMOND AND NUTMEG PRALINE

- 1/3 cup (80 ml) whole almonds
- 1/3 cup (80 ml) whole hazelnuts
- 1/2 cup (125 ml) cane sugar
- 3 tbsp (45 ml) water

DARK CHOCOLATE MOUSSE

- 1 cup (250 ml) 35% cream
- 1 tbsp (15 ml) cane sugar
- 1/3 cup (80 ml) dark chocolate, chopped

INGREDIENTS

ALMOND SUPREME

- 1 cup (250 ml) sliced almonds
- 2 tbsp (30 ml) cane sugar
- 1/2 tbsp (7.5 ml) honey
- 1/4 cup (60 ml) unsalted butter

OPTIONAL FINISHING

- Caramelized hazelnuts (recipe on page 150)

(recipe on page 150)

ALMOND SUPREME

- In a pot on medium-high heat, heat the almonds, sugar and honey for 3 to 4 minutes until the almonds become golden and the mixture sticks to a spoon.
- Add the butter and cook for 2 minutes.
- Pour the mixture onto a piece of parchment paper and cover with another piece of paper. Flatten the hot almonds with a rolling pin to get a thin layer.
- Remove the top piece of parchment paper and let cool for about 10 minutes at room temperature.
- Break the almond supremes into pieces to decorate the pie.

ASSEMBLY

- Cover the crust with the almond and hazelnut praline. Pour the chocolate mousse on top of the praline. Decorate with the pieces of almond supreme and, if you like, the caramelized hazelnuts.

JOSÉE'S RECOMMENDATION

For a perfect matching of flavours and to reduce the sweetness of the praline, I like Mangaro 65% cocoa dark chocolate from Michel Cluizel. Its flavour wonderfully completes the praline.

SAVOURY IDEAS

When I began to work on this book, I wanted it to exude creativity. It became so ingrained in me that it became contagious. I wanted to inspire anyone who liked baking to push their own culinary limits for pleasure. This section on savoury ideas is probably closest to the essence of my intentions. Here, creativity unfolds in multiple ways. There are some suggested paths, and we invite you to breathe new life into them, to transform them into a variety of other delights, or to embellish them with finesse and add character to the recipes. All you need to do is explore and create new recipes with your creativity and daring. A delectable world is at your door. Take pleasure in the process and make it rain puff-pastry discoveries.

Pastry Making Ideas
LEFTOVER PASTRY

What do you do with leftover pastry? Bake it, of course! There are all sorts of quick, easy recipes to bake leftovers in savoury ways. Here are three that do not miss the mark in pleasing everyone.

Nombrils-de-Sœurs
Leftover short pastry
Brown sugar and ground cinnamon

- Make a ball with the leftover dough and roll it out with a rolling pin.
- Dust the brown sugar and ground cinnamon onto the dough.
- Roll up the dough, cut into rounds and place on a cookie sheet.
- Bake them at 350^0C (180^0F) for 15 to 20 minutes, or until they are golden.

Palmier Sticks
Leftover puff pastry
Cane sugar

- Make a ball with the leftover dough and roll it out with a rolling pin.
- Cut out 4 x 3/8" (10 x 1 cm) sticks.
- Spray the sticks with water, roll them in the sugar, twist them and place them on a cookie sheet.
- Bake the sticks in the oven at 350^0F (180^0C) for about 20 minutes, or until they are golden brown.

Sesame Crackers
Leftover puff pastry
Sesame seeds
Salt, pepper or your choice of spices (curry, Cajun, barbecue or other)

- Make a ball with the leftover dough and roll it out with a rolling pin.
- Place the dough onto a piece of parchment paper and brush with water.
- Cover the dough with sesame seeds.
- Salt and pepper and/or season them with your choice of spices.
- Cut into small rectangles of about 2 x 1" (5 x 3 cm).
- Slide the parchment paper with the rectangles onto a cookie sheet.
- Bake at 350^0F (180^0C) for about 25 minutes, or until they are golden brown.

COOKIES

Many of the pie crusts we have developed could be transformed into delicious cookies. Here are some of our favourite suggestions. It is up to you to mix pastries, ingredients and spices of your choice to create others that are just as succulent.

Chocolate and Hazelnut Shortbread Cookies

Sweet chocolate pastry (recipe on page 14)
Your choice of the amount of hazelnut pieces, toasted cane sugar

- Add the quantity of hazelnuts desired into the ball of dough toward the end of the dough mixing (once the dough is chilled, it is harder to make).
- Form a disk of 1 1/4 to 1 3/4" (3 to 4 cm) in diameter with the dough.
- Chill the dough in the refrigerator for about 1 hour or until it hardens.
- Dampen the chilled roll of dough with water and roll it in the sugar.
- Cut the dough into 3/8" (1 cm) slices.
- Bake the cookies through in the oven at 350⁰F (180⁰C) for 15 to 30 minutes, depending on their size.

VARIATIONS

You can replace the hazelnuts with chocolate pieces or other types of nuts.

Butter Shortbread Cookies

Shortbread pastry (recipe on page 15)
Cane sugar

- Roll out the dough to a thickness of 3/8" (0.5 cm) and cut out with a glass or a fluted cookie-cutter (repeat with the leftovers).
- Brush the tops of the dough pieces with water and generously dust with sugar.
- Place the pieces onto a parchment paper-lined cookie sheet and bake at 350⁰F (180⁰C) for 15 to 20 minutes, depending on the size, until the shortbread is golden.

Oatmeal Pecan Cookies

Pecan and oatmeal crust (recipe on page 106)

- Make small balls of dough and lightly flatten them.
- Bake the cookies at 350⁰F (180⁰F) for 15 to 20 minutes, depending on their size.

Crispy Cookies

Cookie dough pastry (recipe on page 15)
Your choice of ingredients (chocolate chips, nuts, dried fruit, candied citrus, spices, etc.)
1 egg, beaten

- Add the quantity of ingredients desired into the ball of dough toward the end of the dough mixing (once the dough is chilled, it is harder to make).
- Make small balls of dough and lightly flatten them.
- Brush with the beaten egg and garnish with nuts or something else to your taste.
- Bake the cookies in the oven at 350⁰F (180⁰C) for 15 to 30 minutes, depending on their size.

GOURMET CHOCOLATE CANDIES

Are you crazy for chocolate? You will love these homemade, easy-to-make candies. Begin with the indicated recipe and follow the steps below. Then let your creativity run wild. Invent more with your favourite pastries!

- Make the recipe as indicated.
- Spread out the dough in a square or rectangular pan or on a cookie sheet lined with parchment paper.
- Follow the baking instructions for each piece of dough.

- Cut or fashion the crust once it is chilled. For the truffles, make balls and roll them in cocoa powder. For the pavés, break the crust into a variety of sizes.
- Keep the candies in the fridge.

Brownie Squares
Brownie recipe from the Indecent Chocolate and Praline Duo on a Brownie (page 122).

Sesame and Sunflower Chocolate bars
Recipe for the crust from the Infinite Delirium of Chocolate, Sesame and Truffles (page 138).

Chocolate Pecan and Coconut Triangles
Recipe for the crust from the Intense Coconut Extravaganza (page 121).

Raisin, Chocolate and Almond Truffles
Recipe for the crust from the Cappuccino Dolce Vita Pie (page 133).

Chocolate Pavés with Puffed Rice and Peanut Butter
Recipe for the cookie in the Chocolate Ice Cream Sandwich Pie (page 105).

Decorative Ideas

Do you love adding a pretty finishing touch to your pies? Whether it's just for pleasure or for a special occasion, here are a few easy-to-make decorations that add colour or flavour to your pies. You can even make them in advance to make it easier. It is up to you which ones will garnish your next pie!

Fruit Crisps

Fruit of your choice (apple, pear, orange, lemon, lime or other)
Icing sugar

- Finely slice the fruit with a mandoline or a serrated knife (use the knife for the citrus).
- Dip both sides of the fruit into the icing sugar.
- Cook in the microwave on high power for 3 minutes, turning the slices every minute (the consistency should be tender).
- Cook in the oven at 175°F (80°C) for about 4 hours, or until the crisps are dry.
- Leave the crisps in the open air for a day so they dry out more then store them in an air-tight container.
- The crisps keep for a week.

DOMINIQUE'S ADVICE

Put the crisps on the pie right before serving so they do not become soggy in the refrigerator.

If you see that the crisps are moist, put them back into the oven for 1 to 2 hours at 175°F (80°C).

Chocolate Curls

1 bar of milk or dark chocolate

- Use a peeler to make thin curls from the longest side of the chocolate bar, starting from the top to the bottom (like a carrot).
- Note that curls made from dark chocolate will be shorter than those made from milk chocolate.

Candied Citrus Zest or Slices

1 to 2 citrus fruit of your choice (orange, lemon, lime)
1 cup (250 ml) water
1 1/2 cups (330 g) cane sugar

Zest

- Make strips of zest with a peeler.
- Cut each strip into thinner ones with a knife.

Slices

- Cut the citrus into thin slices.

Zest and Slices

- In a pot, bring the water and sugar to a boil to make syrup.
- Pour the hot syrup into an air-tight container and add the zest or slices. Close the container tightly and cool at room temperature.
- When it is completely cold, refrigerate for 24 hours.
- Strain the zest or slices. Use to decorate the top of pies to your liking.
- The zest and slices keep in the syrup for a month in the fridge.

Maple Syrup Caramelized Nuts

1 cup (250 ml) nuts
(walnuts, pecans, cashews)
1/4 cup (60 ml) maple syrup

- Preheat the oven to 325°F (160C).
- Roast the nuts in the oven for 15 minutes.
- When the nuts are roasted, turn off the oven but leave the nuts inside.
- In a non-stick pan on high heat, bring the maple syrup to a boil. Turn down the heat to low and simmer for 2 minutes.
- Pour the hot nuts into the maple syrup and cook on low heat, while stirring constantly until the nuts are caramelized.
- Spread out the nuts on a cookie sheet lined with parchment paper and cool.
- Once the nuts are dry, break the clusters if necessary. Use the nuts for decoration or eat them as a snack.
- The nuts will stay dry in an airtight container.

Cane Sugar Caramelized Nuts

1 cup (250 ml) nuts (hazelnuts, almonds, peanuts, pistachios)
1/4 cup (60 ml) cane sugar
2 tbsp (30 ml) water

- Preheat the oven to 325°F (160°C).
- Roast the nuts in the oven for 10 minutes.
- When the nuts are roasted, turn off the oven but leave the nuts inside.
- In a pan on high heat, cook the sugar and water for 3 minutes.
- Mix the nuts in the sugar. Remove from heat and continue to mix for a few minutes to fully coat the nuts with caramel.
- Spread the nuts out on a cookie sheet lined with parchment paper.
- Once the nuts are dry, break the clusters if necessary. Use the nuts for decoration or eat them as a snack.
- The nuts will stay dry in an airtight container.

Fruit Crisps

Chocolate Curls

Candied Citrus Zest and Slices

Maple Syrup Caramelized Nuts

Choco-Banana Indulgences

Exotic Islands

Tricoloured Sticks

Creamy Peanut Pastry

Petit Fours Ideas

Throwing a cocktail party and looking for some good ideas to sweeten up your guests with dessert? Here are five succulent examples of petit fours that you can prepare using the recipes in this book. What begins as an invitation to play with various recipes can lead to all-new dessert ideas that suit your taste.

Choco-Banana Indulgences
- The base of these 1 1/2" (4 cm) small squares is sesame and sunflower chocolate crust (page 138).
- Cover the squares with milk chocolate mousse (page 138).
- To finish, garnish with the caramelized bananas (page 135).

Exotic Islands
- The base of these 1 1/2" (4 cm) diameter rounds is sweet pastry (page 13).
- Cover the rounds with pastry cream (page 82) or whipped cream (page 156).
- To finish, garnish with chopped exotic fruit (kiwi, mango or other).

Creamy Peanut Pastry
- The base of these 1 1/2" (4 cm) diameter rounds is made of puffed rice, chocolate and peanut butter cookie (page 105).
- Cover the rounds with whipped cream (page 156).
- Garnish the whipped cream with toasted peanut pieces or caramelized nuts (page 150).

Tricoloured Sticks
- The base of these 3 x 3/4" (8 x 2 cm) sticks is brownie crust (page 122).
- Cover the sticks with white chocolate mousse (page 130).
- To finish, garnish the mousse with fresh strawberries.

Small Choco-Raspberry Indecencies
- The base of these 1 1/2" (4 cm) diameter rounds is brownie crust (page 122).
- Cover the rounds of brownies with ganache (page 123) or whipped cream (page 156).
- To finish, garnish the ganache with fresh raspberries.

Small Choco-Raspberry Indecencies

Parfait Ideas

Do you have a weakness for parfaits? Have fun creating your own using the recipes in this book. The possibilities are only as limited as your imagination. So, let your creativity soar and move from one recipe to the next to create small, unique, mouth-watering desserts. To get you started, here are five from our collection. They will inspire you to invent a host of others!

Tropical Stopover

Tropical Stopover

- The base is coconut cream (page 121).
- Then, a layer of mango mousse (page 126).
- Coconut crisps are used as a garnish (page 121).

Ruby-Red Velvet

- The base is sweet pastry crumble (page 60).
- A first layer of mascarpone whipped cream (page 137).
- A layer of homemade or store-bought strawberry jam.
- A second layer of mascarpone whipped cream.
- A layer of fresh raspberries on top.

Sunny Mount Chocolate

- A base of milk chocolate mousse (page 138).
- A layer of chocolate crumble (page 129).
- A layer of dark chocolate mousse (page 142).
- Orange supremes on top to brighten it up (page 166).

Adam's Sin

- A layer of caramel mousse (page 102).
- A layer of sautéed apple jam with cinnamon (page 117).
- A second layer of caramel mousse.
- A honey and sesame crisp for a finishing touch (page 139).

Fresh Breeze

- A base of grapefruit gelée broken up with a knife (page 94).
- A layer of diced strawberries.
- A few mint leaves on top for garnish.

Ruby-Red Velvet

Sunny Mount Chocolate

Adam's Sin

Fresh Breeze

Coulis, Sauces and Creams

Do you want to double the enjoyment for you and yours? Top your pies with coulis or cream to add a gourmet and seductive signature that pleases the eyes and the palate. Here are the classics of the genre. You can use them to inspire other delicacies.

Raspberry or Strawberry Coulis

3/4 cup (175 ml) cane sugar
1/2 cup (125 ml) water
3 cups (750 ml) raspberries or strawberries

- Bring the sugar and water to a boil and pour it over the raspberries.
- Mix well with a hand-held blender.
- If you want a coulis without seeds, filter it though a fine-meshed strainer while it is still hot.
- This coulis keeps for two weeks in the refrigerator.

Chocolate Sauce

1 cup (250 ml) 35% cream
1/2 cup (125 ml) dark chocolate, chopped

- Heat the cream without bringing it to a boil and pour over the chocolate.
- Mix well with a hand-held blender.
- Reheat lightly before serving.
- This sauce keeps for one week in the refrigerator.

Caramel Sauce

1/2 cup (125 ml) cane sugar
3 tbsp (45 ml) water
1 cup (250 ml) 35% cream, hot
(read DOMINIQUE'S ADVICE)

- In a pot, on medium heat, heat the sugar and water until a caramel forms.
- Remove from heat. Gradually add the hot cream and mix well.
- This sauce keeps for one week in the refrigerator.

Whipped Cream

1/2 vanilla pod
1 cup (250 ml) 35% cream
2 tbsp (30 ml) cane sugar

- Cut the vanilla pod in half lengthwise and scrape the seeds out with a knife. Put into the cream.
- Whip the cream, vanilla seeds and sugar to stiff peaks.
- Ideally, whipped cream is made right before serving and should be eaten the same day.

Custard

3/4 cup + 1 tbsp (190 ml) milk
1/3 cup + 1 tbsp (95 ml) cane sugar
5 egg yolks

- In a pot, heat the milk on medium high, without bringing it to a boil.
- In a bowl, mix the sugar and egg yolks. Add the hot milk and mix again.
- Put the mixture back into the pot and heat for 2 minutes while stirring constantly.
- Remove from heat and mix with a hand-held blender for 1 to 2 minutes.
- Cool at room temperature.
- Custard keeps for two days in the refrigerator.

DOMINIQUE'S ADVICE

The cream must be hot before pouring it into the hot caramel. If it is cold, there is a risk of splatter that could cause burns. As the saying goes, better safe than sorry.

Gourmet Note

To enhance the taste of the custard, you could flavour it by adding 1 to 2 tablespoons (15-30 ml) of liqueur. Here are some suggestions:

- Rum, to accompany pies with bananas, apples or chocolate;
- Calvados (apple brandy), for pies with apples;
- Grand Marnier, for citrus pies.

Strawberry Coulis

Chocolate Sauce

Custard

Caramel Sauce

Whipped Cream

CULINARY INFORMATION AND TRICKS

This book would not be complete if it did not give you all the information you needed to explore all regions in the pie-making universe. You'll find plenty of tips in this section: cooking instructions, advice, definitions and other information that explains or simplifies things for you when you need it. It also has recipes to help with garnishes. Everything that you need to visit all of our "destinations" is right here!

AGAR AGAR
Purchase

A vegetable substance and red algae extract, it is made of pectin and blooms in water. A vegetarian substitution for gelatin, agar agar is sold in flakes or powder. It is found easily in Asian and health-food stores.

Usage
- Heat 2 cups (500 ml) of liquid (water, juice or other) on low heat at 185°F (85°C). The low-temperature is necessary in order to dissolve the agar agar.
- Pour 1 1/2 teaspoons (7.5 ml) of powdered agar agar or 2 tablespoons (30 ml) of flaked agar agar in the liquid. Bring to a boil, lower the heat and simmer for 5 to 10 minutes until the agar agar is completely dissolved.
- Add it to a mixture immediately, within the recipe's specifications, to set it quickly.

Note

Depending on the type of agar agar you use, the quantity required to thicken could vary. You can determine this through trial-and-error or by following the instructions on the packaging.

APPLES

When you choose apples for a recipe, it is helpful to know that certain varieties are more heat resistant than others. For your pies, use Empire, Cortland, Golden or Lobo apples since they stay intact during baking. To stew or make a sauce, opt for McIntosh apples instead, as they disintegrate quickly when cooked.

CANE SUGAR
Selection

We use cane sugar as it is more natural and less processed than refined white sugar. Brown in colour, it is the product of cane juice that is dehydrated using traditional methods. Be careful of products labelled "brown sugar" as they might actually just contain coloured white sugar. Other than cane sugar, the only sweeteners we use in our recipes are honey and maple syrup.

Method of Adding Sugar by Sprinkling

This operation consists of letting the sugar fall gently, in small qualities, into a mixture, like a gentle rainfall. To do this, take a spoonful of sugar and distribute it by gently shaking the spoon in a circular motion over the preparation.

CARAMEL
Cooking

To succeed in making caramel, you must be very attentive to the cooking time, as it burns quickly when cooked too long.

Caramel turns from translucent to white, then to golden, and finally, to brown. It is ready when it is brown.

If it is black, obviously it is completely burnt. If you want a caramel with a light taste, stop cooking it when it is lightly golden. If you are looking for a caramel with a more pronounced flavour that is slightly bitter, cook it until it is dark brown. In general, North Americans prefer a light caramel and Europeans, a stronger flavoured caramel. A little tip for cleaning: when you have finished your caramel, boil water in a pot containing all the utensils you used. It will melt the stuck caramel and facilitate cleaning.

SOFT CARAMEL

The key to success is to add hot cream at the right moment when there is no more water in the mixture and the colour turns from golden to brown. The density of the steam coming out of the pot will be an indication. When there is little water left, the steam becomes opaque and so the colour changes. Hot cream should be added when the colour of the mixture turns pale or dark brown, depending on your taste. Once the desired colour is obtained, you should add the hot cream and take the pot off the heat right away. The cream must be hot so it does not seize the caramel. Cold or warm cream can also cause splashing and burns.

CRUNCHY CARAMEL

To make crunchy caramel, continue cooking for 3 to 5 minutes once the cream is added, or until the caramel becomes very thick. Once the cream is added, the taste will no longer change (unless you continue to cook the caramel for more than 5 minutes after adding it). Spread out the caramel onto a piece of parchment paper and let it harden at room temperature. When it has hardened, break it into pieces to use in your recipes. You can even eat it as is and let it melt in your mouth.

CHOCOLATE
Purchase

When you are choosing chocolate, it is important to be familiar with the significance of the indicated percentages on the packaging. It will give you information on the quantity and intensity of cocoa products used in the making of the chocolate. So, a chocolate of 70% cocoa means that it uses 70% cocoa products including cocoa butter and cocoa solids (also called cocoa paste or liquor). Normally, only products made with cocoa butter can be designated as chocolate. The lower the percentage, the lighter and sweeter the chocolate tastes. The higher it is, the more intense and bitter the taste of chocolate. You should also consider that the first item on the list of ingredients is always in the greatest amount in the product.

DARK CHOCOLATE

Principally, chocolate is made of cocoa and sugar. Depending on the percentages of ingredients included in the production, taste can vary between light and strong. Cocoa content mostly varies between 55% and 70%. Sugar counts for almost the rest of the percentage. Most people prefer chocolate with 55-60% cocoa. Dark chocolate, also called unsweetened, bittersweet or semisweet, is the most authentic form of chocolate.

MILK CHOCOLATE

Milk chocolate is made of cocoa products, sugar and milk, and cream or milk powder. It should contain less than 25% cocoa products and 12% milk solids. The taste is sweeter than dark chocolate and the colour is paler as well.

WHITE CHOCOLATE

White chocolate is made of cocoa butter, sugar and milk and one or more flavours, most often vanilla. White chocolate does not contain cocoa solids. The ivory colour of the product comes from the cocoa butter, which is a vegetable fat. It is obtained by pressing the cocoa beans, which generally have an ivory-yellow colour (it can also be closer to brown).

Selection

We don't specify the cocoa content of chocolate in our recipes because we prefer to let you make the choice to use the chocolate that better corresponds to your taste. I did, nevertheless, make recommendations for certain recipes where the chocolate was a key ingredient. Globally, we recommend you use chocolate made by artisan or established chocolate makers with a known savoir-faire, such as Michel Cluizel, Valrhona or Cacao Barry. Their products are made with choice ingredients, their cocoa beans are specially selected and they use respected and refined methods. You can find these types of products in gourmet and speciality boutiques. To help guide you with your choice of chocolate, we offer a list of chocolates that we like to recommend.

RECOMMENDATIONS FROM CACAO BARRY

The chocolates from Cacao Barry are generally found in small disk form in boxes of 1 kg. Some speciality boutiques offer smaller packages for home use.

Origins Line	Characteristics
Tanzanie	• Dark chocolate 76% cocoa • Intense and acidic taste, mild accents of spices and fruit
Saint-Domingue	• Dark chocolate 70% cocoa • Very pronounced taste, fruity and exotic notes
Mexique	• Dark chocolate 66% cocoa • Bitter and acidic taste, delicate hint of licorice
Ghana	• Milk chocolate 40% cocoa • Characteristic taste of hazelnut with a hint of caramel
Plantation Line	**Characteristics**
Alto El Sol (Peru)	• Dark chocolate 65% cocoa • Extended taste with fruity accents and a clear hint of acidity
Oropucce (Trinidad)	• Dark chocolate 65% cocoa • Intense, strong cocoa taste, light fruit and wine flavours
Madirofolo (Madagascar)	• Dark chocolate 65% cocoa • Balanced taste, fruity, acidic and a unique mild bitterness
Chocolate Couverture	**Characteristics**
Bittersweet Favourites	• Dark chocolate 58% cocoa • Lightly sweet and spicy taste, with strong and persistent aromatic flavours

RECOMMENDATIONS FROM VALRHONA

Valrhona chocolate comes in bars. The Grands Crus line is presented in cardboard packaging and the original line is sold in paper packaging.

Grands Crus Line	Characteristics
Abinao	• Dark chocolate 85% cocoa • Tannic and strong flavour, very bitter and delicately acidic
Guanaja	• Dark chocolate 70% cocoa • Assertive and bitter taste, with a light acidity and pleasurable flavours
Alpaco	• Dark chocolate 66% cocoa • Intense and bitter taste, floral, woody and grilled, dried fruit accents
Caraïbe	• Dark chocolate 66% cocoa • Balanced flavour, voluptuous, bitter and lightly acidic, with notes of grilled, dried fruit
Manjari	• Dark chocolate 64% cocoa • Fresh taste, acidic and fruity with a delicate aroma of grilled, dried fruit
Taïnori	• Dark chocolate 64% cocoa • Taste marked by grilled, dried fruit with fruity and acidic notes
Jivara	• Milk chocolate 40% cocoa • Creamy cocoa taste with a short bitterness
Tanariva	• Milk chocolate 33% cocoa • Mild taste, caramelized and balanced
The Original Line	**Characteristics**
Extra Bitter	• Dark chocolate 85% cocoa • Very full-bodied taste with a defined bitterness
Bitter	• Dark chocolate 71% cocoa • Pronounced flavour with a mild bitterness
Dark	• Dark chocolate 56% cocoa • Balanced taste, light sweetness
Milk	• Milk chocolate 40% cocoa • Unctuous taste, mild and sweet

RECOMMENDATIONS FROM MICHEL CLUIZEL

Michel Cluizel chocolates come in bars. When you use these chocolates, Michel Cluizel recommends lowering the amount of chocolate indicated in the recipes by 10%, since they make the chocolate from the whole bean without decomposing it. The quantity of cocoa butter is higher in these chocolates, giving them a higher chocolate content.

Grandes Teneurs en Cacao Line	Characteristics
Grand noir 85%	• Dark chocolate 85% cocoa • Intense taste, persistent on the palate
Noir de cacao 72%	• Dark chocolate 72% cocoa • Elegant taste, full-bodied and extended in the mouth
Grand lait 45%	• Milk chocolate 45% cocoa • Generous taste, with caramel and hazelnut notes
1ers Crus de Plantation Line	Characteristics
Los Anconès (Saint-Domingue)	• Dark chocolate 67% cocoa • Flavours of licorice root, red fruits and green olives with subtle notes of currants and apricots
Vila Gracinda (São Tomé)	• Dark chocolate 67% cocoa • Taste of toasted spice and herb accents mixed with flavours of ripe tropical fruit and licorice root
Conception (Venezuela)	• Dark chocolate 66% cocoa • Taste nuanced with vanilla, gingerbread and caramel with extended accents of dried fruit mixed with dark fruits
Mangaro (Madagascar)	• Dark chocolate 65% cocoa • Taste very perfumed with exotic fruits with flavours of gingerbread and acidic notes of citrus
Maralumi (Papua New Guinea)	• Dark chocolate 64% cocoa • Roasted and spicy accented taste with fresh notes of green banana, flavours of red currant and subtle aromas of Cuban tobacco leaves

QUICK GANACHE

Here is a succulent recipe for quickly made ganache suggested by Didier Girol, the Quebec ambassador for the house of Michel Cluizel.

It is just as good to cover the bottom of a pie as it is to eat as a spread.

1/3 cup (80 ml) 35% cream
1/2 cup (125 ml) Maralumi chocolate, chopped
2 tsp (10 ml) white rum

- Cook in the microwave for a maximum of 1 minute and mix.

CITRUS
Thin Peels

This operation consists of removing the peel and the white pith from the fruit with a knife to leave the pulp naked.

Removing Supremes / Sectioning

Peel the citrus and take out the pulp from between the membranes with a sharp knife.

Removing Zest

Begin with washing the skin of the citrus well. Often, citrus peels are covered in pesticides. To zest, use a very fine grater like a Microplane, to remove the coloured skin of the fruit where there is a concentration of essential oil, and consequently, aroma. To make zests, meaning fine strips of peel, use a zester or peeler to get long, thin bands. The thickness will vary depending on the utensil you use. In any case, avoid removing the white pith as it is bitter. Zest serves, above all else, to perfume and decorate.

EGGS (WHITES)
Usage

Separate the whites from the yolks when the eggs are cold. Let the whites rest at room temperature and make sure the whisk and bowl are free of any traces of fat before whipping them.

Method of Whipping (Soft Peaks)

Use a whisk with numerous thin wires to maximize contact between the egg whites and the whisk. Beat the whites at medium speed in a mixer, to avoid beating them too much, until the consistency is firm and light, all without sticking to the whisk. Gently take the whisk out and leave it detached in the bowl. Use beaten egg whites in your recipe as quickly as possible. This method is used to make cakes such as sponge cake.

Method for Stiff Peaks

Beat the whites at medium speed in a mixer, ideally with a thin-wire whisk. Gradually add sugar while whipping, until the texture thickens. When the whisk is taken out, the mixture should stay stuck and form long, stiff peaks that resemble swan beaks. The more sugar added to the mixture, the more consistent and stiff the peaks will be. Whipped egg whites beaten to stiff peaks are used among other things, to make meringues.

Meringues

To succeed at making meringues, the egg whites must be whipped to stiff peaks.

The secret to success is to add the sugar gradually

and gently in a thin stream when the whites go from clear to white during whipping. Continue whipping until stiff peaks form.

EGGS (YOLKS)
Method to Lighten in Colour

Vigorously whip the eggs with sugar until the mixture turns pale. The eggs are lightened when the sugar dissolves and the pale yellow colour is closer to white. This step only takes a few minutes, but is important. It creates volume in recipes and stops lumps from forming when a hot liquid is added to the mixture.

FLOUR
Advice

As supporters of a healthy diet, we recommend baking with unprocessed, unbleached flours, as natural as possible, rather than flours with added baking soda or any other chemical agent. It goes without saying that the recipes in this book were created uniquely with unprocessed unbleached flour. In fact, the only flours we use and offer at Première Moisson are specialty natural whole-wheat flours without chemical inputs, made entirely with wheat cultivated in Quebec in the flour mill of Moulins de Soulanges. This company, which Première Moisson co-owns, along with Meunerie Milanaise, which specializes in milling organic grains, and Agrifusion, a group of wheat producers, has as their mission the crafting of superior quality commercial natural flours and speciality flours adapted to the needs of artisan bakers. These companies ensure the compatibility of the traceability of wheat, total control of the product, respect for the environment and economic development. At Première Moisson, we are invested in this endeavour. As our business philosophy, we wish to concretely participate in the betterment of the food chain.

Selection

In Quebec, all-purpose flour is the most common in stores. It can be used for baking, pastry making and bread making. It is also the favourite choice for all our pie pastry recipes. This type of flour is, in a way, a flour of compromise that is found between white bread flour (type 55 or T55 in France) and white pastry flour (T45), which is lighter and used for fine pastries (brioche, croissant, puff pastry, etc.). In the baker's shop, four other kinds of flours are used: white flour without additives (T65) with which traditional French white bread is made, wheat flour (T80), whole-wheat flour (T110) and wholemeal flour (T150).

FRUITS
Advice

All our recipes are made with fresh fruit. Because we like to celebrate the wonders Mother Nature offers, we recommend you always use seasonal fruit to make your pies. Not only will you discover the beauty of living in symbiosis with nature, but your final products will also be more flavourful. If you are like us, you will quickly get a taste for seasonal food and take advantage of fresh produce while it is naturally available. At a time when everything is increasingly pushed into storage transformed, exported and imported, isn't it appropriate to get closer to nature and live more harmoniously with it?

GELATIN
Purchase

Gelatin is sold in powder or sheet form. The most common gelatins found in stores in Canada are 7 g packages of powder. In Europe, 2 g sheets of gelatin are preferred by pastry chefs. In these recipes, the results are the same, but the method of usage changes. It is important to know that gelatin burns easily, so do not overcook it.

Simplified Usage (powder)
- Pour contents of one envelope of gelatin into 2 tablespoons (30 ml) of cold water.
- Let bloom for 5 minutes and add to the mixture depending on the recipe instructions.

Simplified Usage (sheets)
- Cover four sheets of gelatin with cold water and let bloom for 5 to 10 minutes (four 2 g sheets replaces one 7 g envelope).
- Drain the sheets between your fingers and add to the mixture depending on the recipe instructions.

Note

If you compare the manufacturer's instructions on the box to ours, you will see that we do not mix the powder in boiling water. Although it is often preferred to dissolve powdered gelatin this way, tests that we have conducted have determined that it is more effective with cold water. For the same reason, we used only 2 tablespoons (30 ml) of cold water (instead of the three often asked in the maker's instructions). The simplified usages we have given are based on the tests that we have conducted. Even though different from the manufacturer's, they both yield excellent results and limit excess liquid in our recipes.

GINGER
Preserving

The best way to keep ginger root is to peel and freeze it. It will keep for several weeks. On a shelf in the refrigerator, ginger keeps for two or three weeks. Do not put it in the vegetable crisper. It will get mouldy because of the humidity. We use fresh ginger in our recipes because it is much more aromatic than powdered ginger.

Grating

Freezing ginger makes it easier to grate. Take out a peeled piece, grate it without defrosting and put it back in the freezer. That's it. Quick and easy!

NUTS AND SEEDS
Optimizing Flavour

To get the most flavour out of nuts and seeds, it is preferable to toast them slowly for a long time in a preheated oven on low heat rather than to roast them quickly on high heat. In any case, do not toast them too long or they will have an unpleasant taste. Also note, walnuts and pecans go rancid quickly once they are toasted. We suggest toasting nuts and seeds close to when they are to be used.

Toasting Methods
Slowly: 1 to 2 hrs at 250F (120°C)
Quickly: 15 to 20 min at 325F (165°C)

Preserving

Raw nuts and seeds keep very well in the freezer. When they are toasted, allow them to cool in a dry place before preserving them. Place them inside an air-tight container with a lid.

PARCHMENT PAPER

To keep parchment paper in place when you are lining a pan or cookie sheet, lightly spray the surface of the pan or sheet with water, or grease it.

TOPPING
Usage

Toppings make fruit garnishes shine and gives them a sweeter taste.

Method

The simplest way to make a topping is to use store-bought apple or red fruit jelly or apricot jam. Heat it to a liquid and brush the amount of your liking onto the fruit of your pies. You can also make your own topping. We have proposed a recipe below. This topping keeps for several months in the fridge.

Honey Topping
1 cup (250 ml) honey
3/4 cup (75 ml) water
1 package (7 g) gelatin

- Bloom the gelatin in 2 tablespoons (30 ml) of cold water for 5 minutes.
- Boil the water and honey together for 5 minutes. Remove from heat.
- Add about 1/4 cup (60 ml) of the hot mixture to the gelatin and pour the mixture into the rest of the hot honey and water. Mix with a whisk.
- Set aside in the fridge.

Usage
- Heat the topping when it is time to use it.
- Brush the fruit garnish with a brush.
- To have a thick topping on the fruit, let it chill in the fridge until it is a semi-firm consistency, but still liquid enough to be brushed on.

UNSALTED BUTTER
Advice

We stick to using unsalted butter to be able to control the amount of salt in our recipes. If you only have salted butter, reduce the quantity of salt in the recipe to your taste.

VANILLA
Bought

There are more than fifty varieties of vanilla. The most renowned are from Réunion and Tahiti. When you are buying vanilla, look for thick, supple, dark pods. Little white crystals that appear on certain varieties are a sign of quality. These crystals are natural crystallized vanillin from the fruit. It is an integral part of the aroma. Vanilla is also sold in powder and liquid extract. Use only pure vanilla products as they clearly have a better flavour than artificial products.

Usage

In our recipes, only the seeds are used. To remove them, cut the vanilla pod in two lengthwise and extract the seeds by scraping the pod with the tip of a knife. Vanilla is also used to scent sugar or infuse liquids. Here are recipes to make your own pure vanilla extract.

Vanilla Sugar
1 cup (250 ml) cane sugar
1 vanilla pod

- Put the sugar into a jar with an air-tight lid.
- Split the pod lengthwise and cut it in half widthwise. Add the pod to the sugar.
- Close the jar with the lid and shake to mix.
- Let the sugar infuse with the vanilla for two to six weeks (the longer the infusion time, the more the vanilla will perfume the sugar).
- Shake the jar twice a week so the flavour is evenly distributed.

Note

For vanilla sugar, it is not necessary to use an entire pod. An empty vanilla pod without seeds will give the same results.

Infusion
1 vanilla pod
2 cups (500 ml) milk or cream

- Remove the seeds from the vanilla pod. Add the seeds and the pod into the liquid.
- Heat for 20 minutes without bringing it to a boil (the longer it infuses, the more it is perfumed).
- Remove the pod once the infusion is finished. It could give the liquid a bitter taste if it stays in too long (keep the pod to make vanilla sugar).

Homemade Pure Vanilla Extract
1 cup (250 ml) pure alcohol or vodka 37 to 40%
100 g vanilla pod

- Pour the alcohol or vodka into a bottle (ideally, an opaque bottle).
- Remove the seeds, cut the pod into three or four pieces, and add everything to the bottle.
- Put the bottle in a dark area for about six months.
- Shake the bottle two or three times for the first two weeks and once or twice per week thereafter.
- After 6 months, filter the extract through a fine mesh strainer to remove the seeds and pod.
- The extract will keep for many years and improve with time, like with wine.

UTENSILS

PANS

All pans are not equal. Certain pans allow for a better bake than others, depending on the materials used in fabrication. Others have properties that simplify the work. Here's some information to help you choose.

Cast-Iron Pan

Cast-iron diffuses heat progressively to the whole surface of the pan. This not only allows for a uniform bake, but also keeps the food hot when it comes out of the oven.

Ceramic or Porcelain Pans (3)

These materials support and distribute heat very well, favouring an even bake. Pans made with these materials can go from the oven to the table easily. They are an excellent choice for baking pies.

Dark-Coloured Metal Pans

Dark-coloured metals absorb heat well and favour browning. Pans made in this fashion are excellent for baking crusts.

Fluted Tart Pans with Removable Bottoms (2)

The removable bottom facilitates turning out pies. You simply have to push the bottom upwards in order to turn out the pie without deforming it. The fluting gives a pretty look to the pie. This type of pan can be found in many dimensions. It is well-suited for baking pies.

Light-Coloured Metal Pans

Light-coloured metal pans do not hold heat. Pans that are made this way are not good for baking crusts or pies.

Metal-Coated Silicone Pan

This new generation of silicone offers all the advantages of the previous, but also allows crusts to get a crispy texture. Cooking with this pan can also take 20% less time than traditional silicone pans.

Non-Stick Pans

Non-stick surfaces are very practical to turn out pies as they stop the dough from sticking to the pan, which keeps pies intact. This kind of pan helps pies bake well.

Cookie Sheets

A cookie sheet is an essential tool for baking certain crusts. It absorbs and distributes heat over its total surface, allowing for a uniform bake. Chose cookie sheets with sides because they keep parchment paper and pies in place when taken out of the oven.

MEASURING INSTRUMENTS

Measuring instruments aren't always of the same quality. The actual value of measurements isn't always exact and can vary from one tool to another. If you cook a lot, we recommend you invest in a kitchen scale to weigh your ingredients as chefs do.

Candy Thermometers

An instrument that takes precise temperatures of preparations to achieve perfection. Some models attach to the side of pots; others rest on the side of them. When you take temperatures, all that matters is that the thermometer comes in contact with the mixture so that you can have an exact read.

Pyrex Pans (4)

Pyrex holds and distributes heat well, which permits crusts to brown. Pans made with Pyrex are multipurpose as they withstand heat as well as cold. A favourite choice. They create more golden and crisp crusts.

Silicone Pans

Silicone assures a uniform bake but inhibits the crust from getting a crispy texture. It is smooth and polished. Flexible, non-stick and heat inhibiting, the pans allow the pies to turn out easily, preserving a nice appearance. When they come out of the oven, they are not as hot and can go straight into the freezer.

Springform Pans (1)

This kind of pan is ideal for making tall pies. It favours impeccable baking and it is easy to turn out pies.

Kitchen Scales (5)

There are many automatic and electronic models. A good kitchen scale will let you measure your ingredients with more precision. This tool is also ideal for converting exact imperial to metric measurements, and vice versa.

Measuring Cups for Liquid Ingredients (7)

They are distinguished by their spouts to help with the use of liquids. The full measurement is shown under the top of the cup to avoid spilling. Generally, they are graduated in quarters and thirds of the full measurement (1/4, 1/2, 3/4, 1/3 and 2/3 cup for a one-cup container). They can also be graduated in millilitres.

Measuring Cup for Solids (8)

The full measurement comes to the very top of the cup. If the cup is too full, the top can be levelled by running a straight object, such as a knife, over the

Blender (12)

Electronic appliance with a base, speed controls and a rotating knife with a few blades. It has a vessel with a handle, spout and lid. This sits on the base and mixes ingredients to make homogeneous liquid preparations of different thicknesses.

Eggbeaters

Manual hand-held tool with a hand crank and two whisks with four paddles on each, used to aerate beaten egg whites.

Electric Hand Beater (9)

Hand-held lightweight electronic tool with speed controls and two whisks with four paddles, each one able to beat egg whites, whip cream or reduce butter and sugar into a cream.

Food Processor (15)

Electronic appliance with a crankshaft, speed control, a detachable stem, blades or discs, a bowl with a handle, a lid with a feed tube and a tamper. It cuts, grinds, minces, shreds, chops, slices, kneads or mixes solid ingredients to prepare them or make mixtures of different consistencies.

Hand-Held Blender (Immersion Blender) (14)

Lighter and more compact than eggbeaters, this streamline electric appliance can plunge directly into a vessel (bowl, pot or other) to whip, emulsify, liquefy, blend or purée food. It is very handy for mixing a small amount of something. It is often sold with an adapted container.

top to remove the excess in order to have an exact measurement. The base measurements normally include four pieces: 1/4 cup, 1/3 cup, 1/2 cup and 1 cup.

Measuring Spoons (6)

Essential for measuring ingredients in small amounts. The standard sets consist of four spoons: 1/4 tsp, 1/2 tsp, 1 tsp and 1 tbsp.

MIXING TOOLS

In cooking, there are many ways to prepare ingredients and mixtures, though some are harder to accomplish by hand. Thankfully, human ingenuity has developed a series of tools to facilitate things. Most of the ones we describe here have become essential, especially for creating desserts.

Mixer (Stand Mixer) (11)

Electronic appliance with a hinged head where a whisk or a dough hook (two on some models) can be attached, which adds, blends, mixes, beats, whips and aerates solid and liquid ingredients at variable speeds, in a bowl on the base to obtain homogeneous preparations of different consistencies. Some high-end models have an adjustable bowl.

Pastry Cutter (13)

A "U" shaped stainless steel utensil attached to a wood or plastic handle. The bottom is comprised of five or six parallel blades slightly curved to help incorporate flour and solid fat, most often butter, without having to use your hands, which would cool down the mixture. The term pastry cutter is also used for a rectangular metal block, sometimes rounded at the end and attached to a handle used to cut or lift pastry. It can also be used as a scraper.

Whisk (10)

Manual base utensil with many metallic wires, used to beat or mix a preparation or to boost the volume of a solid ingredient by incorporating air.

OTHER TOOLS

To be efficient in the kitchen, it is important to use the right utensils to complete the right tasks. Here is a list of other principal utensils that can help you succeed with the recipes in our book.

Apple Corer

Tool comprised of a handle on one end and a curved blade with a cylinder that cuts at the other. It is used to remove the core of certain fruits, such as pears and apples.

Channel Knife (see Zester)

Cooling Rack

A rack that is slightly raised on feet, which accelerates cooling of pies.

Double Boiler (Mixing Bowl) (16)

Master tool for pastry chefs, this half-circle receptacle, which is often made out of stainless steel, helps make preparations. It can serve as a bain-marie with a pot to melt chocolate and is available in different sizes.

Grater (Like a Microplane) (21)

A tool with a handle and tiny "U" shaped blades that finely grate ingredients. A must have to zest with extreme finesse.

Mandoline (19)

A flat tool furnished with cutting space that easily prepares fruits and vegetables in slices, rounds or julienne in different thicknesses.

Melon Baller (17)

A utensil with a handle on one side and a hollow half circle on the other, which is used to remove small balls of melon flesh. It can also be used to remove the cores of certain fruits.

Parchment Paper

Paper treated to be waterproof and heat resistant to high temperatures. It is used in the kitchen to stop food from sticking to cooking utensils and facilitates turning out prepared foods and cleaning.

Pastry Brush

A tool that brushes pastry, crust and fruit garnishes with water, beaten eggs, topping, etc. You can choose from models made of natural silk or silicone.

Peeler (18)

A small tool that has a blade with a large gap in the middle that pivots (and can sometimes be removed from the pivot on some models.) It is used to easily peel vegetables or to remove the zest from citrus by following their shapes. Certain models have blades that can also make decorative patterns.

Plastic Wrap (Cling Wrap)

Thin, plastic film that is impermeable, adhesive and elastic, depending on the brand. We use it in some of our recipes for lining the bottom of pans to facilitate turning out pies.

Piping Bag and Tips (20)

Tool made of a watertight conical pocket. At the end, a removable decorative tip can be attached. This utensil gives decorative forms to soft preparations. The set usually contains a few decorative tips.

Pot

Cylindrical utensil with a handle, often with a lid, that cooks on the elements of a stove. For uniform

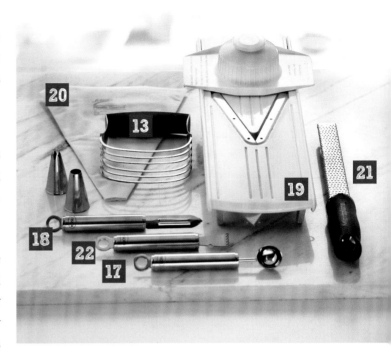

cooking, use thick-bottomed pots as they provide better heat diffusion. It is always convenient to have at least a large and a small pot in one's kitchen.

Rolling Pin

Cylindrical tool of a variable size, sometimes furnished with lateral handles, which rolls out dough. Traditionally, rolling pins were made of wood, but newer models made from stainless steel, silicone, polyethylene or with a non-stick surface are making their mark. It is an indispensable tool for making pies.

Sifter

Cylindrical tool with a fine-meshed net. It serves to remove lumps from solid ingredients, such as flour, icing sugar and baking powder. Certain models are activated by a manual mechanism. Sifters are also used to dust icing sugar for a finishing.

Spatula

Another tool essential in pastry making, the spatula is like an extension of an arm, adapted for cooking. It has a handle and a flexible, rectangular paddle that is flat on the end and sometimes rounded in the corners. It is mainly used to scrape the corners of bowls and pots, to mix ingredients, to fold in preparations, to spread and smother toppings and so much more. There are many models of spatulas and each one has its function. The most common models are made of rubber, wood, silicone and metal.

Strainer

Receptacle with holes, with or without a handle, which drains food. Or a tool with a handle, frame and round netting, more or less fine, which filters mixtures or sifts or dusts dry ingredients.

Zester (22)

Tool with a handle fashioned with a curved blade with five sharp perforations used to remove long filaments of zest. One side cuts to remove fine strips of peel without removing the pith of the citrus. Some zesters come with a channel knife—a blade containing a "V" shaped opening that is used to cut strips of citrus zest.

Glossary

Baking a Crust Through

Long bake on low heat so the crust is cooked through, without a burnt taste.

Blind Bake a Crust

Short bake before adding the filling. To stop it from puffing up, it is covered with parchment paper and dried peas before putting it in the oven.

Cannelé Bordelais

Small, soft cake fluted in a cylindrical form.

Chop

Cut, with a knife or other sharp tool, into small pieces.

Core

Remove the core of a food (e.g., core an apple).

Coulis

Raw fruit puree, filtered through a strainer and used to top pies and other desserts.

Crumble

Crumbly sweet dough made up of fine and large pieces. It also means to work the ingredients of a pastry with the tips of your fingers in a way that the pastry will obtain a texture similar to that of sand. This technique is used for short and shortbread pastries.

Crush

Smash an ingredient to reduce it to pieces, more or

Crust

Piece of dough rolled out with a rolling pin to make the bottom of a pie.

Docking the Pastry

A step that consists of making small holes, normally with a fork, in a pie crust to stop it from inflating during baking.

Dust

Cover with a thin layer of a powdery substance, such as icing sugar.

Emulsify

Vigorously whip two liquids that normally would not mix by introducing a fat, so that they mix homogeneously. Whipping renders the heavier of these two liquids into microscopic drops and suspends them with the other liquid to make a mixture that appears uniform.

Flute

The crease or small cavity in the wave of the fluted pan (pan with sides in a repetitive "S" formation).

Fluted Pan

Pan with ringed sides that make small longitudinal cavities.

Folding

Add one delicate preparation into another by turning one over the other with a spatula without any brisk motions.

Follicle

Dried fruit opened up to expose its content. Each branch of a star anise is a follicle.

Grease a Pan

A step that consists of covering a pan with a fat, generally butter, before putting a crust or a preparation into the oven. It impedes it from sticking.

Grinding

Reduce an ingredient to minuscule particles under the force of pressure or repetitive shocks, like with the food processor, for example.

Line the Pan

Cover the inside of a pan with rolled-out pastry to constitute a pie crust on which the filling will be poured or placed, depending on the composition.

Line with Parchment Paper

Synonymous with "cover with parchment paper."

Quenelle

Small, oblong (more long than wide) shapes, formed with two soup spoons by passing mousse from one spoon to the other until you obtain a perfect quenelle (see photo on page 119).

Scallop

Join the edges of two pie crusts (the top and bottom) by creating a scalloped edge—a decorative border in the form of waves.

Sift

Filter a solid ingredient through a sifter or strainer to remove the lumps (consult the terms "sifter" and "strainer" in the "Utensils" section).

Spiral

Curve that forms a coil.

Star Anise

A brown spice in the form of a star with eight branches. The strong scent is very characteristic. Among other things, it is used to flavour desserts and jams, and it is used in the making of pastis. As an herbal tea, it is known for its digestive properties that help reduce bloating and flatulence.

Stew

Cook for a long time on low heat to get a jam-like texture.

Supreme

A portion of pulp found between, and removed from, the membranes of citrus.

Sweetener

A substance that gives a sweet flavour, such as sugar, honey and maple syrup.

Topping

Cover with a jelly, coulis, sauce or other similar substance.

Acknowledgments

Josée's Acknowledgments

I would like to say an enormous thank you to my mother and my brothers for their immeasurable confidence in me and for their understanding that I was less available at Première Moisson as I worked on this book. Special acknowledgments also go out to my daughter Anne, for all her discerning comments and her little fairy-like fingers that kneaded dough with me so well, and to my son Nicolas, the gourmet's gourmet, who always took pleasure in savouring my creations. Thank you to Gilles and Jade for their support, for sharing my enthusiasm and for all the wonderful times spent together around this delicious apple pie...nom, nom!

Thank you to all the friends of my children, Félix-Antoine, Émile, Camille, Cléo and Thomas who tasted again and again my numerous pies during the entire summer.

Thanks to Aline and Henri for the inspiration and passion they filled me with.

Thanks to the whole team that supported me during this intense, magical adventure:

Julie, Louise, Christian, Éric, Véronique, Line, Min, Donna, Manon and Lillian.

Thanks to Pierre, Nino, Luce, Jacques and Guy from Studio Tango for all their excellent work (a special thank you to Jacques for his collaboration on certain recipes).

Thank you to Éditions de l'Homme, and to you, Erwan, for your unfailing support.

Thanks to you, Dom. I had such pleasure writing this book with you. And, finally, thank you life. You must bite right into it, like an apricot pie!

Dominique's Acknowledgments

I would like to thank:

Josée for thinking of me as a co-author and sharing with me her endless stream of stimulating reflections, which were the heart of this book;

Première Moisson, the wonderful company where it is so easy to evolve;

Min, for being my loyal number two through the conception of these recipes;

Louise and Julie for their diligence in testing numerous pies;

Véronique and Donna for the delicious moments of tasting;

Lillian, for her due dates and her sweet strictness;

Eric, for his precious and appreciated advice;

the team at Studio Tango, Luce, Jacques and Guy, for their superb photos;

les Éditions de l'Homme, for believing in us;

and, finally, to my wife and my son, for their understanding and their priceless presence in my life.

Thank you to you all, for all the fabulous moments shared with passion and delight.

Notes